THE FULLNESS IN HIM

A JOURNEY OF TRANSFORMATION

MARITZA BARRON

The Fullness in Him: A Journey of Transformation

Print ISBN: 979-8-9863062-2-3

Printed in the United States

THE FULLNESS IN HIM

A JOURNEY OF TRANSFORMATION

MARITZA BARRON

ENDORSEMENTS

"We are incredibly blessed to be part of Maritza's life. She carries the love and joy of the Lord in such a unique way. This book is full of wisdom, the Word, powerful prayers, and testimonies that will bless you. We pray that Maritza's journey will help bring transformation in your life as you experience more of the fullness in Him."

- Aaron & Beth Packard; Firestorm International, Author of Reckless Surrender

"Maritza does an incredible job helping her reader come closer to Jesus through her words. With stunning imagery and scripture to back her storytelling, it will be hard to put this book down. If you are looking for a study that will lead you to truth and the love of Christ, this Bible study is it! I warmly commend it!"

- Nicole Rowan; Mother of 5, Founder of Revival Women

"This incredible book reveals essential keys for fostering a deeper relationship with Christ, inviting you to embark on a transformative journey through scripture, prayer, and self-discovery. Whether you are a seasoned believer or just starting your faith voyage, this resource will illuminate a step-by-step path to a more profound and fulfilling walk with Jesus. For scripture says, "for we walk by faith, not by sight." 2 Corinthians 5:7 ESV"

- Amy Dudley; Author, Speaker, Spiritual Gangsta

"For everyone in any season, *The Fullness in Him*, will transform your understanding of what it truly looks like, biblically and spiritually, to live in the fullness of God. Walking in faith, love, confidence, and wisdom of who God has called us to be. Maritza's poetic words and personal stories paint a picture of our identity in Christ and what living in His fullness looks like. It's not a destination we arrive at but a journey we partner with the Lord in as we grow. Thank you, Maritza, for this beautiful book!"

- Desiree Siegfried; Author, Host of Do You See podcast, and founder of Prayer Doves

ENDORSEMENTS

"*The Fullness in Him* is a book written to help lay a biblical foundation in the life of believers. Throughout the pages, you will find not only insightful thoughts and personal experiences from the author, but you will find each chapter pointing you back to Scripture to learn the fullness of what Jesus Christ has already provided for you through his life, burial, and resurrection. This book will help you not only gain fresh perspective but if you allow the Holy Spirit to work with you as you read it, you will be encouraged to find the freedom and strength you need to walk out your new identity, but also, find true wholeness and healing in Christ."

– Christine Morgan; Founder of Worldwide Evangelistic Ministry

"For years now the Lord has placed before me the revelation of Spiritual fullness. As I dig through the Word of God I'm both stirred and awestruck upon the reality of seeing the Church shine as she enters into the promise of *the fullness of the stature that is in Christ (Eph 4:13).* Could it be that in the last days God's people will shatter boxes of limitation through their Divine union with Christ?

Individually, a metamorphosis readily stands before us in Christ like an open door, drawing us into transformation and change for his glory. No person remains the same once experiencing a touch from God. Christianity is unique from other faiths in that through Christ we are not only forgiven of our trespasses, being made right in the eyes of God; we are also changed on a supernatural level in our very nature. A new creation in Christ.

I want to heartily endorse Maritza Barron's new release; *The Fullness in Him.* I've known Maritza for a few years now and have witnessed her faith and compassion serving on overseas missions teams together. She lives to see Christ glorified and his power present to cause the lost reconciled to God.

The book you're holding in your hands is a rich well of revelation. I like that it's Christocentric and I thank God for more voices rising up like Maritza who will herald the pure gospel message that offers wholeness to the reader.

The Fullness in Him will woo you into his presence of God chapter by chapter. Like deep which calls to deep. You will be blessed and glad you sowed into your journey of transformation in Christ by reading this book."

– Alex Parkinson; Evangelist, The Zion Company Intl. Author, Spirit Without Measure

ACKNOWLEDGMENTS

First and foremost, I want to thank the Lord for walking with me and never giving up on me. For giving me the fullness of His life unto eternity, I am forever grateful.

Thank you to those who have encouraged and prayed for me during this process. To the Ennis family, for providing the time and space where the writing and creativity could freely flow.

The Brown and Leeth family; thank you for opening your home to me, a complete stranger. I am blessed to be able to now call you family. Your love and joy make an impact on those who have the privilege to meet you!

Antoinette; your time, the hours on the phone in prayer, in tears, and in laughter have been invaluable! You are a God-send.

The Packards; where do I start? Thank you for your faithfulness to the Lord, the wisdom you share, your patience with me, and for seeing the gift in me when I couldn't! May the love of the Lord keep increasing in your lives unto overflow, swimming in His goodness, drinking of His joy! More Lord!!!

CONTENTS

MESSAGE FROM MARITZA:

Dear Brother/Sister in Christ,

First and foremost, I want you to know that I am extremely humbled and honored that you would allow me to speak into your life, to encourage you, and help you grow in Him, our King, Jesus Christ.

This book you have in your hand is not just a normal book. And, while it is written in a bible study format, it isn't just another bible study. These pages you are embarking on came about through the tests and trials of life. As I sought to know Him more, He kept revealing more of Himself. In a life where I just wanted to be loved and have an amazing life of adventure, I would only find counterfeits, which led to much frustration. Jesus pursued me and soon consumed me. To be consumed can mean: to be completely destroyed or to absorb all of the attention and energy of someone.

Indeed, He completely destroyed my old life full of fear of many sorts. He also came to absorb all my attention and energy, filling me with hope and joy for the future.

My prayer is that through this study you come to a place where all your attention and energy will be absorbed by Him and vice versa. That He will fill you with all of Him and consume you with His holy fire, if you let Him. My desire is that you get revelation through this book and truly understand what it means to be in Him, how you can live your life in Him, and where you firmly believe He is your everything.

With Love in Him,
Maritza Barron

PS: Since this is written in a study format, this is an interactive book. You will find parts asking you to look up scripture, and questions for you to answer. Plan to have your Bible with you as you read this book. You will get out of this as much as you put into it. I pray Holy Spirit will guide you and lead you.

CHAPTER 1

BEGINNING IN HIM

Then He told them, "These are My words that I spoke to you while I was still with you—that everything written about Me in the Law of Moses, the Prophets, and the Psalms must be fulfilled." —Luke 24:44

IT IS FINISHED . . .

After six hours of hanging on the cross, Jesus took the sour wine and, with His last breath, declared, "It is finished." Then he bowed His head and gave up His Spirit (John 19:30).

This moment right here carries exceedingly and abundantly more for you and me as sons and daughters in Christ. This moment opened up a whole new world for us, a whole new dimension, a whole new realm.

I opened my prayer journal this morning and reflected on the graphic in the center of the page. The picture looked like a door or even a window, but what I heard in prayer was, "A gate!" Yes, a gate! The image of this gate had vines growing over it. In my imagination, I walked through the gate. On the other side, it was full of light and wonderful, beautiful flowers of various sorts of colors, sizes, and fragrances. It was so lush and vibrant on the other side of the gate. It was full of life.

I was reminded of a provoking inference spoken in a documentary on the Iranian church, *Sheep Among Wolves*: "A graveyard has perfect order, but in nurseries, there is life." There is a nursery, a garden that carries life that is waiting for us to step into. This is what is on the other side of that gate—life.

Where is that gate? The question is probably more like, *Who is that gate?* And then how do we get to the other side? There is only one way, and His name is Jesus. He is that gate for all who wholeheartedly believe.

You see, on this side of the gate, we only imagine perfect order. Just as the documentary inferred, perfect order is found only in our graveyards, not in the world of the living. On this side of the gate, fear of the unknown often leads us to hold too close to the familiar, and our best-laid plans loom over us like death shrouds taking our souls captive. We can compare fear to a graveyard, a valley of dry bones where there is no life. But there is hope on the other side: "In the nurseries, there is life." We must choose to step *through* the gate to enter a new life full of adventure in the unknown, into the place of being wowed, surprised, and awed.

All this talk of gardens reminds me of the movie *The Secret Garden*, which could only be entered by those who had a key. There is also a garden for us with God, our own Eden, back to His original intention: a life of purpose, power, and province.

The key to this new beginning is with Jesus at the cross.

AT THE CROSS

"When Jesus had received the sour wine, He said, 'It is finished!' Then bowing His head, He gave up His Spirit" (John 19:30 HCSB).

It may sound cliché, but in reality, it's true. The end of something is the beginning of something new. This is why, in believing in Him, all things are made new. "Therefore if anyone is in Christ, he is a new creation; old things have passed away, and look, new things have come" (2 Corinthians 5:17). Jesus' death opened a door for us to live a new life. This is exactly the journey we will be taking, going to that new and original creation.

So we must ask ourselves now: When Jesus said, "It is finished," what was finished?

We will find that what was finished, indeed, was the war over darkness and sin. Scripture also tells us that death is the wage of sin (Romans 6:23). Jesus conquered death at the cross. It is only HIS death that brings life to us. What are things that bring death? Yes, sin, but let's think here. Disease, worry, fear, and hopelessness are just some examples of mechanisms that bring death to the body and to the soul. Nevertheless, sin brings death to our very being.

BUT JESUS . . . He conquered death.

> Now since the children have flesh and blood in common, Jesus also shared in these, so that through His death He might destroy the one holding the power of death—that is, the Devil—and free those who were held in slavery all their lives by the fear of death. —Hebrews 2:14–15

Jesus surely destroyed death and the devil. Let's look at another scripture in Colossians:

> And when you were dead in trespasses and in the uncircumcision of your flesh, He made you alive with Him and forgave us all our trespasses. He erased the certificate of debt, with its obligations, that was against us and opposed to us, and has taken it out of the way by nailing it to the cross. He disarmed the rulers and authorities and disgraced them publicly; He triumphed over them by Him. —Colossians 2:13-15

In this physical world, there are times when we feel like we are dead in life as if we are walking around with no purpose and no life in our souls. This is exactly what Jesus came to destroy on the cross—anything and everything that brings death to you and me.

Listen, the debt has been paid! The word used in the Greek for "it is finished" is *tetelestai*, which means "paid in full." Jesus paid it all for us with His precious blood and cleansed our sins away. As Colossians 2 says, "He erased the certificate of debt." There is nothing else we must do to "pay back" our debt; we can't even get close to paying anything back, even if we tried. Jesus did it all on the cross. It is by *faith* we receive this gift of not just salvation but all that is given to us by His sacrifice, which is a life in Christ in all its fullness.

Let's look at a section in Scripture that describes what happened at the cross.

> He was despised and rejected by men, a man of suffering who knew what sickness was. He was like someone people turned away from; He was despised, and we didn't value Him. Yet He Himself bore our sicknesses, and He carried our pains; but we in turn regarded Him stricken, struck down by God, and afflicted. But He was pierced because of our transgressions, crushed because of our iniquities; punishment for our peace was on Him. And we are healed by His wounds. —Isaiah 53:3-5

Go back to that scripture of Isaiah above and circle all Jesus took for us and write them below:

____

____

If we keep reading verses six through twelve, we will find there is more Jesus took for us at the cross. We will find He was oppressed, afflicted, and judged for us. We will also discover He was struck because of our rebellion. Jesus took all the oppression, affliction, and punishment on the cross so we don't have to bear it in our souls in this life or the one to come. He did it because He loves us.

Going a bit further, we see Jesus bore and finished two other wounds that often affect us in this life: those are pain and suffering.

About three years ago, I was in a season of facing pain and rejection. As I spent time with Jesus, I recall telling Him through all my tears about how what I was going through was "so painful." Quite honestly, I even said I didn't want to keep going anymore; I wanted to give up. I felt like my heart was being ripped apart; I couldn't bear it anymore.

At that moment, Jesus said to me, "I know, and I don't want you to carry it anymore. I have done it for you." And then He showed me a vision in my mind's eye. I saw Him sitting on the bed right in front of me. Then, I heard Him tell me I needed to face the thing that was causing my pain. He showed me how I had avoided feelings of rejection and had hidden them deep inside of me. He said, "Maritza, if you are willing to face this pain, it will surface, and you can give it to me. I will take it from you because I already bore it on the cross; it's not yours to keep."

I had to make the decision to either hold on to pain or give it to Him. I chose to trust Him and began the journey of giving Jesus all the pain of rejection I stuffed away.

In Scripture, Jesus Himself tells us we will have suffering in this world, but we can be courageous because He has conquered the world (John 16:33). You may now be pondering how Jesus took pain and suffering on the cross, yet He also said that we will have suffering? Well, let us look up Revelation 21:4 and Matthew 6:10 and write them out below:

By putting these scriptures together, we can see that in God's dwelling place, the heavenly realms, there are no more tears, no more death, and no more grief and pain because the old has passed away. We covered previously that when we become a new creation in Christ Jesus, God Himself comes to dwell within us by His Holy Spirit. This is the first step in allowing the scripture of Matthew 6:10 to become reality, bringing heaven to earth.

First, let me briefly mention a bit about Holy Spirit. In John 14:17, Jesus calls Holy Spirit the Spirit of Truth who will come to live inside of believers. John 14:16 says, "And I will pray the Father, and he shall give you another Comforter, that he may abide with you for ever" (KJV). John 14:26 says, "But the Comforter, which is the Holy Ghost, whom the Father will send in my name, he shall teach you all things, and bring all things to your remembrance, whatsoever I have said unto you" (KJV).

Romans 8:26 says, "Likewise the Spirit also helps in our weaknesses. For we do not know what we should pray for as we ought, but the Spirit Himself makes intercession for us with groanings which cannot be uttered" (NKJV). And Galatians 5:22-23 tells us, "The fruit of the Spirit is love, joy, peace, patience, kindness, goodness, faith, gentleness, self-control." John 16:33 says, "I have told you these things so that in Me you may have peace. You will have suffering in this world. Be courageous! I have conquered the world."

What I want to communicate is, as a believer, you have the indwelling presence of God's own Spirit. You also have all the personality traits and fruit of the Spirit within you. We may experience moments of suffering, but it is no longer something that should keep us down in a place of despair, in a graveyard of dry bones. In these moments of suffering, we may depend on the Holy Spirit, the Comforter, to comfort us and, therefore, bring His peace. This is how we can experience heaven on earth and "no pain," which Revelation 21:4 explains. So now is the time to receive His truth, His grace, to live an abundant life. We don't have to wait until we get to heaven to experience heaven on earth in the fullness of His joy.

I will add this: If you are currently experiencing pain from the past, this is meant to surface from where it was buried so that you no longer carry burdens in your heart. Jesus is right there beside you, waiting for you to give your burdens to Him. He is the burden bearer.

One last point about what happened at the cross. He took the curse—the curse that was meant for us. Galatians 3:13-14 reads: "Christ has redeemed us from the curse of the law by becoming a curse for us, because it is written: Everyone who is hung on a tree is cursed. The purpose was that the blessing of Abraham would come to the gentiles by Christ Jesus, so that we could receive the promised Spirit through faith."

Look here—Jesus was hung on a tree, nailed and hung, blood dripping and falling into the earth to restore you and take the curse of this fallen world so that you don't have to stay there. This is what Jesus came to do, to restore us to the original state that we were intended to live in, which is the Garden, metaphorically speaking—the state before Adam and Eve sinned. This means that if the devil has been torturing you and calling you cursed, you can choose to believe that what Jesus did on the cross is for you. You have the power to fight back with the Word of God in the power of the

Holy Spirit. Scripture says that an undeserved curse goes nowhere (Proverbs 26:2), which means when you become a new creation in Christ, you shouldn't be living in any sort of cursed life. You have the access and the ability to live a life here on earth free of all the bondages and curses of the fallen state because Jesus redeemed you from it on the cross.

I must really emphasize here that what Jesus has done has turned our world right side up. What He has finished on the cross brought us to our rightful place and dominion, and when we understand this, we come to realize all the negatives in our lives are actually a bunch of lies from the devil, the lying serpent. You see, he is the one who is truly cursed. He is the one who will never get to live in the light, never have full authority and dominion. Because of his demise, he tries to get you to believe you are the one cursed. We see this same story with Absalom, David's son, who hung from a tree by his hair after he tried to steal the throne from David. Satan tried to steal God's throne, so now he is cursed. Now he is trying to steal your throne!

Before you move on, take the time to write down below the answer to this question: What did Jesus finish at the cross for you?

THE GREAT EXCHANGE

Let us pause and thank Jesus for what He has done for us. It is this great exchange at the cross where He finished our battle, where He took every wound that brings death to us. What He gave us in return: His body and His blood, His life.

This is the place where we exchange our brokenness so that we can have His broken body and His innocent blood, and with these, we become whole. Brokenness is vulnerability, and when we are vulnerable, we are open to receiving. When we come to Him in our brokenness, in a posture of vulnerability and a place of weakness, it is at this moment His strength and His love can come into our lives, into the places we can't possibly begin to know how to heal. Yet He does, and He has; all we need to do is receive. *He comes in our weakness because this is when we have no strength to resist Him.* We are able to open our hearts and allow Him to work.

As for the blood, there is so much power in the blood. First and foremost, the blood in our bodies is what carries life; without blood in our bodies, we are dead.

This is also true with the blood of Jesus—it offers life. The blood of Jesus is pure and was shed for our atonement. His blood is potent and without blemish. Take note of this: In the book of Luke chapter 23, Jesus is taken to Pilate to be charged, but Pilate himself said he found no grounds to charge him. Here we are in the legal courts, in the earthly realm, where the authorities announced that Jesus was innocent. His blood was pure and holy, the perfect sacrifice. His blood cleanses us and purifies our blood into gold. Each time you claim His blood, and you commune with it, there is a blood transfusion that happens. His blood dominates our earthly blood, stumping all generational curses. We come into the bloodline of Jesus.

As we learn to commune with Jesus in deeper intimacy, we manifest His life more and more within us. This is that new life we talked about earlier once we step through the gate named Jesus. It is through faith we are saved; through faith and by faith, we also step into Jesus and pick up what He came to give us, as John 10:10 says, a life to the fullest:

> I am the gate; whoever enters through me will be saved. They will come in and go out, and find pasture. The thief comes only to steal and kill and destroy; I have come that they may have life, and have it to the full.
> —John 10:9-10 NIV

MADE NEW

This is where it begins: your new life in Him. "Therefore, if anyone is in Christ, he is a new creation; old things have passed away, and look, new things have come" (2 Corinthians 5:17). As we go through these pages, you are heading into a revelation of all you are in Him—a journey of learning what it means to have the fullness of life, the fullness of Christ Jesus.

You will be leaving the old behind and learning to walk into your new self in Him as the person He originally created you to be in Him. You will be stepping into the original intention, where you will be better than before, back to the place of "as if it never happened." Back to Eden, walking with God, being in His presence, into eternity.

Each day, as you go through this journey, you will be made more like Jesus! It is where we say, "All of me, Jesus, for all of You." We learn to let go of the past and step into Him. We will understand to see like He sees, think like He thinks, talk like He talks, act like He acts. We are going from glory to glory throughout the pages. We are to be completely consumed by Him and become one with Him. Just as Scripture says, we are to walk just as He walked. So we are going to walk as He walks.

THE ULTIMATE GIFT

Bear in mind the way God created you to be and to walk in this life is by receiving the gift through the cross. There was a third gift Jesus gave us at the cross besides His body and blood, and I already briefly mentioned this gift: Holy Spirit. It is by this gift we gain the ability to come into the abundance and the full life of Christ. Without Holy Spirit, we do not have the supernatural power to walk in the fullness of Jesus in us.

"But you will receive power when the Holy Spirit has come on you, and you will be My witnesses in Jerusalem, in all Judea and Samaria, and to the ends of the earth" (Acts 1:8). Holy Spirit is the One who will give us the power and fire to be consumed by God and to receive all the fruits of the Spirit and the wonders of the Lord, for it is by the Spirit that we will come into the place of fruitfulness in the Garden. It is by the Spirit that we inherit the fullness of God, breaking out of the stagnancy of life and complacency of the mindset that tells us, "Well, we are saved, and we don't need to do anything else; we will just wait for Jesus to come back." Holy Spirit teaches us all things and shows us just how to step into this new life in Him with the fullness of who He is.

The invitation is here! Step in the gate—into life.

> "I am the door. If anyone enters by Me, he will be saved and will come in and go out and find pasture." —John 10:9

Are you ready?

PRAYER

Jesus, thank you for the cross. I want to break free from the bondage of death and step into the life you came to give me. I choose to believe in you and in all you have for me. I step through the gate today. Send me your Holy Spirit and teach me to walk in your ways. Amen.

CHAPTER 2

FAITH IN HIM

Now faith is the substance of things hoped for, the evidence of things not seen. —Hebrews 11:1 KJV

Faith is a very important matter of our journey. It is required to walk in heavenly places with Jesus while on this earth. When Jesus said, "On earth as in heaven," He was exhorting us to live now in the fullness of God, in Him. Faith is so simple and yet so profound to us that we often miss it. Hebrews 11:1 states, "Now faith is the substance of things hoped for, the evidence of things not seen" (NKJV). In a society that relies on physical evidence and scientific data, faith is often difficult to put in perspective. But God asks us to believe in the faith that is fully alive in the unseen realm of God's promises.

As I sit here this morning staring at the whiteboard in front of me and reading in all capital letters, "FAITH LIKE GEORGE MÜLLER," I am reminded of a season in my life when I needed to live completely by faith. George Müller was a giant of the Christian faith, a man from the eighteenth century who dared to trust God to answer his prayers, not only his own needs but the needs of many orphans. George Müller was an evangelist in England who built orphanages for children who lost their parents to the cholera epidemic hitting England, leaving many children as orphans. By faith, he built the orphanages, and, by faith, he was able to feed them and care for them—all because he believed in the power of prayer and had faith in God. I would call him a giant of the faith. At the time, I was about to start a faith walk of my own, one in which God had called me to leave my job. I needed to have faith that He would provide for those around me and for me in every area of my life. In this season, I was faced with the reality of a faith journey that God would require of me.

Faith: Faith is required to walk in Him.

Look up Hebrews 11:6 and write it below:

I want to encourage you to seek the Lord about this lesson of faith because the book journey ahead will require us to walk together in unity of understanding. First of all, the verse says, "Without faith it is impossible to please God."

"Why?" You may ask. Because anyone who comes to Him must believe that He exists and that He rewards those who earnestly seek Him. We are embarking on a walk of faith, one of stepping into an unseen realm in Him. God is faithful to His Word and will do what He says, but only when we partner with Him will we start to walk in the life Jesus intended for us.

It is written, "Look, his ego is inflated; he is without integrity. But the righteous will live by faith" (Habakkuk 2:4). For it is only BY FAITH that we can live this new life Jesus freely gave us—His life. "And I no longer live, but Christ lives in me. The life I now live in the body, I live BY FAITH in the Son of God, who loved me and gave himself for me" (Galatians 2:20, emphasis mine). Because we said yes to Jesus and accepted His atoning life, we are now crucified in Him. As we put one foot in front of the other and keep moving forward, we pick up His life by faith.

It is *by faith* that every person mentioned in Hebrews chapter 11 got to be in this portion of Scripture. Go read this chapter and write what each person did by faith:

Abel:

Enoch:

Noah:

Abraham:

Sarah:

Isaac:

Jacob:

Joseph:

Moses:

Rahab:

Since there is an abundance of insight in this passage, I'll start by highlighting how every person had faith to believe in something that was beyond themselves. Noah, for example, was a man motivated by godly fear to build the ark that would deliver his family and many generations to come. There is another in this chapter of Hebrews whose faith made them righteous, Abraham. We can see through these men of huge faith that God does not require perfection—He only requires us to believe in the promises that go beyond what our earthly minds can comprehend. The next piece that grabbed my attention is how Scripture mentions, "Moses persevered as one who sees Him who is invisible" (verse 27), and Sarah "considered that the One who promised is faithful" (verse 11).

It is only BY FAITH in Christ that we can live the supernatural life He gave us at the cross—to believe in the unseen and believe in who God is. As we keep exchanging our old selves for the new in Him, it is only by faith we will live the rest of our lives if we want to fully live the supernatural life.

Jesus Christ and the Word of God are the solid foundation on which we can stand: our unfailing truth, full of faith, living and active in all of those who believe.

GOD REMAINS FAITHFUL

There is something about faith I want to first make you aware—that *God remains faithful no matter what.* I briefly mentioned earlier that it is our responsibility to have faith and partner with His Word. Be aware that even if we don't believe Him or partner with Him, His Word still remains; we just won't be part of that life.

God is so good. He is faithful. Even when we sin and won't partner with Him, He is willing to give us what He has promised—but at a cost—without His presence.

Before we look at the Word, I want to share my own experience with this for you to see what I mean. My biggest desire was to be married and have children. One day, when I was in a travailing prayer about this promise, I clearly heard the Lord say, "Maritza, you could have been married when you wanted, but tell me, where would I be?" Immediately, I knew what God was saying. I knew the answer to that question, and I knew deep down that He would not have been part of my life, my marriage, or my family. His presence would have been far from me. He showed me that day that chaos would have flooded my life if I had proceeded with any kind of marriage that was born out of rebellion, unworthiness, or blatant sin. It would have been a promise fulfilled outside His will and without His presence. That day, He exposed the golden calf of marriage, which needed to be destroyed, so I could walk in faith with expectancy, seeking Him and no longer seeking a husband. I needed to have the faith that He has spoken His promise over me and is waiting for me in the land flowing with milk and honey, full of His presence and favor.

Let us now look at what the Lord responded to Moses after Israel had created a golden calf, an idol, to worship instead of worshiping the Lord. The people of Israel had just committed a grave sin: Read Exodus 33:1-4.

The Lord tells Moses, "I will give it [the land He promised to Abraham] to your offspring. I will send an angel ahead of you and will drive out the Canaanites, Amorites, Hittites, Perizzites, Hivites, and Jebusites. Go up to a land flowing with milk and honey. BUT I will not go with you" (Exodus 33:1-3, parenthetical and emphasis mine).

The Lord shows that He keeps His word! What we learn and observe in this passage is that when the people of Israel built the golden calf to worship, what they actually did was put their affection and trust in this idol. They decided in their hearts to not trust the Lord because Moses DELAYED in coming down from the mountain. We see this decision in Chapter 32 of the book of Exodus, where the subtitle of the section in my Bible is entitled "Faithlessness." The Israelites had lost faith in the Lord because of this delay.

It is usually during this time of delay that most people decide to turn away from God, to stop trusting Him, or to give up on their promise. God will keep His promise, but if we put our trust, our faith, in something else and not Him, we live a life without His presence.

Further, we see in Exodus 33:15 that Moses asks the Lord for His presence. Moses did not want to proceed without the Lord's presence because he knew the power and beauty of His presence, that the Lord's presence is what makes us different and distinguished from all other people.

Moses had seen and experienced the glory of God; he tasted and saw. Moses took the invitation to behold the Lord face-to-face, unveiled. Because of this, he even got full of the glory of God, which gave him the capacity to go without food or water for forty days and come away with the glory of the Lord shining on him. He radiated with the presence of the Lord everywhere he went. We can say Moses lived a supernatural life, having experienced the glory of the Lord Himself, which is why he did not want to go further without God's presence.

IN HIS PRESENCE

In His presence is where all the wonder happens. It is where we become distinguished and different, where we become a peculiar people. Yet it is also in His presence that our faith grows, and our own logic is silenced so that the Lord can speak and move in ways that make no sense to us, in ways that let the Spirit jump within us. It is in this place we are transformed and taken from glory to glory and become unshakable, just as Jesus is.

Let's look at the story of Hannah. Hannah was a childless woman who had a rival that would taunt her for not conceiving. Scripture tells us that Hannah would go to the Lord's house and cry to the Lord with many tears. Notice this next scripture: "While she continued praying in the LORD'S presence, Eli watched her lips" (1 Samuel 1:12). I absolutely LOVE reading this section right here. That scripture tells us that Hannah continued praying IN HIS PRESENCE.

How many times do some of us do one or more of the following when we feel like Hannah did—forgotten, afflicted, hurt, or even experiencing a time of delay:

- Complain
- Get angry
- Stop praying
- Conclude that God is not faithful
- Turn to other idols or comfort
- Give up completely on our promise or God-given desire
- Take matters into our own hands

Take courage. Look at verse 15 and write down what it was that Hannah responds to Eli.

It says that Hannah poured out her heart before the Lord. Now, how beautiful is this? The Lord asks for empty vessels and rendered hearts. It is in this moment, as we keep seeking the Lord in His presence, as we keep pouring our hearts out to Him, that we empty ourselves, allowing Him to move. It is in His presence, in Him, that we are renewed and refreshed. As new life comes, more faith comes. In one of the Bible studies I lead, as we spoke on faith, the Lord revealed to me that THE ultimate act of faith is to seek Him. No matter what is going on, no matter the circumstances, we seek Him and continually do so. We keep going to Him. That even when we don't get what we thought we ought to have received as a reward, we still seek Him. At the end of the day, we must remember that HE is the ultimate reward.

It is what Hannah did. And because of her faith in the Lord, she gave birth to

Samuel, a prophet to the nation, the prophet who would later anoint David as king, the king who is part of the bloodline of Jesus the Messiah. In 1 Samuel chapter 2 verse 5, during Hannah's praise to the Lord, she says that the woman who is childless gives birth to seven. It makes me wonder if she eventually gave birth to a total of seven children, above and beyond what she asked for. Seven, by the way, is the number for completion and wholeness, and there are also seven spirits of the Holy Spirit (Revelation 4:5), which is the fullness of God. This is what our faith is intended to bring: fullness and wholeness to us.

Before we move on, let's look at one more insight on Hannah...Take a look at her name.

HANNAH

Notice how this name is written the same when read forward and backward. Also, if you put a mirror in the middle of her name, you will read Hannah. The very day that a friend of mine revealed this to me, I was in worship and heard, "I want to see the one I love face-to-face," and I also heard Moses cry from Exodus 33:18, "Please, let me see Your glory." Instantly, in my mind's eye, the Lord put a mirror right in front of me. Know this: We are a reflection of Him; this is what this is all about, stepping into the fullness of Jesus, that we walk in Him and reveal Him for all to see. Hannah remained in Him and reflected Him, reflecting His grace, His mercy, His faithfulness, and His glory. The more we commune with Him and spend time with Him in His presence, the more we become like Him.

One of the meanings of the name Hannah is "experienced anguish to break through, to birth the promise in the spirit."

By faith, we give birth to the promise the Lord has spoken.

WAITING IN HIS PRESENCE

Speaking about birthing, this journey is, in essence, all about birthing the promises of the Lord in our lives. We are to birth the destiny of the lives God gave us, which is done by faith—that the seeds He planted in us would grow into fullness so that we may display His glory.

Again, there is nothing like the presence of the Lord. I had to learn this myself. As mentioned earlier, with the story of Moses and the Israelites, they saw that there was a delay in Moses coming down, so they built an idol. It is in this time of delay, also known as "the waiting," that our faith is built and strengthened if we don't give up.

When the Lord started speaking to me about the waiting, I was not excited. In fact, I joked with my friends that this sounded like a horror movie: "The Waiting." What I have learned is that it is the complete opposite; what happens in this season is amazing and beautiful. Let me start by sharing the following scriptures that God highlighted all in one day:

> "Wait for the Lord; be strong and courageous. Wait for the Lord."—Psalm 27:14

> "Be silent before the Lord and wait expectantly for Him." —Psalm 37:7

> "Wait for the Lord and keep His way, and He will exalt you to inherit the land."
> —Psalm 37:34

Now, as you may imagine, for someone who felt like the waiting had been so long already when these scriptures were given to me, I knew God wanted to talk about the waiting. That word "wait" was screaming at me. So when this happened, I grabbed my other Bibles to see what the wording was in other versions. In awe, I read the same scriptures in different translations:

> Don't give up; don't be impatient; be entwined as one with the Lord. Be brave and courageous, and never lose hope. Yes, keep on waiting—for he will never disappoint you! —Psalm 27:14 TPT

> Quiet your heart in his presence and pray. Keep hope alive as you long for God to come through for you. —Psalm 37:7 TPT

> Stop for Yahweh, and travail for him. —Psalm 37:7 ARTB

> So don't be impatient for Yahweh to act; keep moving forward steadily in his ways, and he will exalt you to possess the land.
> —Psalm 37:34 TPT

Look at these scriptures and underline the words that replaced the word "wait."

The two words that stood out to me in the other translations replacing the word "wait" were "travail" and "be entwined as one." This is when I realized what the waiting is really about. It is about being entwined as one with Him. It is going to Him in communion with Him and praying in His presence like Hannah did. I learned that going to pray is travailing for Him! The word travail means "to labor involving painful effort" and "birth pang." To let this really sink in, I had a conversation with someone about this who happened to be a midwife assistant. What this person shared was that as the mother is waiting during pregnancy, the baby is entwined with the mother as one until it is time to come out—until it is time for the birthing. The mother travails, and the mother is expectant!

To clarify, know that waiting is not a time to sit and wait. This season is where something deep is happening in our spirit. As we are being entwined with Him, we are being fed with spiritual food. It is also not just for us to be entwined with the Lord. The child, the calling, the promise must also be one with God for it to come into the full glory of God. As we wait, we become one with Him so that we may keep pressing forward in expectation of the promise in Him. As we wait in His presence, our faith grows stronger because we come to know Him as the true and faithful one.

There are some of you reading this that are in the waiting—waiting for promises fulfilled yet being entwined. This waiting may be hard but be encouraged that, just like Hannah, God will come through because God is faithful. I want to expose a tactic right now of the enemy. We have read this scripture before (John 10:10), but I want you to write it down below:

Why am I having you write this scripture out? I want you to look at the whole scripture and not just at the part that everyone quotes, which is only the ending. Look, God tells us in the first part of the verse that the devil comes to kill, steal, and destroy. God already revealed the enemy's plan, but if we hold fast to the end, the last part of the scripture promises that Jesus came to give us life. My encouragement to you at this moment: Don't abort, don't allow the miscarriage to happen; carry this baby to full term, full of His glory.

What promises are you carrying?

FAITH WORKS BY LOVE

> For in Christ Jesus neither circumcision nor uncircumcision accomplishes anything; what matters is faith working through love. —Galatians 5:6

I remember reading this verse during the time that God was speaking to me personally about faith. I parked on this verse for a while, mainly the last section: *faith working through love.* In this passage of Scripture, Paul is talking about living a life in the Spirit and not in the law—that it's not through works that we get to wherever it is we are trying to get. It is about living a life walking in love and, most importantly, walking a life loving our God. Scripture tells us that God is love (1 John 4:8). We worship, pouring out our lives to Jesus, to the God who is love. Let's go one step further and read the following:

> For this is what love for God is: to keep His commands. Now His commands are not a burden, because whatever has been born of God conquers the world. This is the victory that has conquered the world: our faith. And who is the one who conquers the world but the one who believes that Jesus is the Son of God? —1 John 5:3-5

If I could insert a ton of fire emojis here, I would!!! WOW. I pray you are feeling Holy Spirit's presence the way I am right now as I write that verse! We show our love to God through keeping His commands, through keeping His Word, and through following His Word. Faith works through love. Then the verse tells us that the victory that conquers the world is our faith! The one who believes that Jesus is the Son of God is the one who has conquered the world because of faith in Him! I will be covering in a later section more about keeping His commands when we talk about obedience.

LIFE BY FAITH

We started this section on "Faith in Him" by talking about how we, as spiritual beings, as new creations in Christ, are to live by faith. I'm going to have you look up Galatians 2:20 and write it in the space below:

This verse is crucial for this whole walk in Christ Jesus. I will refer to it a few more times in later chapters. But notice right now that it says, "I live by faith in the Son of God." This is a staple verse because it shows "by faith," we will live "in the Son of God," which really is *in Him.*

> For in it God's righteousness is revealed from faith to faith, just as it is written: The righteous will live by faith. —Romans 1:17

By faith. Understand this: Just as we go from glory to glory, as we continue to walk with Him, we grow our faith and go from faith to faith. What we learn is that to really walk fully in Christ, in Him, we truly must come to a place where we live by faith wholeheartedly.

It begins with a mustard seed of faith. Matthew 17:20 says:

> "Because of your little faith," He told them. "For I assure you: If you have faith the size of a mustard seed, you will tell this mountain, 'Move from here to there,' and it will move. Nothing will be impossible for you."

What does this mean? Where is this seed? The seed is in you! If you are reading this, I promise you it is already planted in you. A seed is planted in you by hearing. Look up Romans 10:17 and write it below:

Faith comes by hearing, and when we are talking about the faith of God, we see in that verse that it is by hearing through the message about Christ. You have heard the message of Christ; the seed is planted.

I have always said that I don't have a green thumb; of course, yes, I am always up to learning, but I do know this— in order for a seed to grow, it needs to be watered, it needs sunshine, it needs good soil, and yes possibly even fertilizer. Let me say this: If faith comes by hearing, this means that repetition is important for us to not only remember but to have a verse come alive in us! This is the diligence, the watering, the sunshine; it is being in the Word. All we need is faith as big as a mustard seed.

Hebrews 11:6 tells us that it is impossible to please God without faith and that He rewards those who diligently seek Him, draw near to Him, and believe He exists. There is an active duty of ours to seek God, to read His Word, and to commune with Him— that we may grow that seed and that we may witness it flourish into the abundant fruit in our lives.

There is action needed on our part. We must act on our faith, when we believe we act upon what we do not yet see. Eventually, we do have to act. It is by faith we will move on what we have heard. In Joshua 3:13, we read that God told Joshua he was to cross the Jordan River, and the priests were to get their feet in the water. In my Bible translation, it says that they were to come to rest in the Jordan's waters, and then the waters would be cut off. The priests had to believe and have faith to step into the Jordan. They had to act on what they heard to see the miracle of the waters opening up for them. Who knows, but I believe that if they didn't set foot in the waters, the waters may have never been cut for them to cross on dry land. They had to make the first move for the Word of God to go forth.

In short, this is faith: Settling it in our hearts that God will do what He said He would. That He is the true and faithful One.

Truly, I believe the Lord wants us to walk in such bold faith that we will genuinely live out what is written in Hebrews 11:33-35!

> Who by faith conquered kingdoms, administered justice, obtained promises, shut the mouths of lions, quenched the raging of fire, escaped the edge of the sword, gained strength after being weak, became mighty in battle, and put foreign armies to flight. Women received their dead—they were raised to life again. Some men were tortured, not accepting release, so that they might gain a better resurrection.

Personally, I also desire to walk like Enoch did. Enoch is in the Giants of Faith Hebrews 11, as you read earlier. Well, Genesis 5:24 says that "Enoch walked with God; then he was not there because God took him." Enoch loved God so much he spent time with Him, walked by faith, and obeyed the Lord. God was so taken by him that He eventually just took him, and Enoch never tasted death. We can learn so much from Enoch. I desire to be one who takes God's breath away—that He may be so delighted in me because I walk with Him.

> Dear friends, although I was eager to write you about the salvation we share, I found it necessary to write and exhort you to contend for the faith that was delivered to the saints once for all. —Jude 3

Remember, you already have the faith in you; it's time to exercise it.

PRAYER

Lord, thank you for your faithfulness. Help any unbelief in me and increase my faith to believe what you have said. I want to please you with my faith. Just as Moses, I want your presence in my life. Grow my desire to be in your Word to water the seeds you have planted in me. Amen.

CHAPTER 3

PEACE IN HIM

Peace I leave with you. My peace I give to you. I do not give to you as the world gives. Your heart must not be troubled or fearful. —John 14:27

"Peace, be still!" These are the words Jesus spoke in Mark 4:39, followed by "and the winds ceased and there was a great calm" (NKJV).

It is time we enter into the peace Jesus came to give us. It is time we speak to our storms with the authority we carry in Jesus and say, "Peace, be still." We may read this verse and think about the physical storm, winds, and weather, which, yes, we can speak to them too, but we need to do the same with the internal chaos that may be happening in our minds and hearts. We must speak, "Peace, be still," to our own hearts and minds.

It is during these storms of life we rise, we fall, we come into our peace, or we allow the storms to crush us. The storms of life can shake us to the core and disrupt the good plans the Lord has for our lives, so we must command them to come into the stillness and the peace of Christ Jesus.

BE STILL

Be still; we must learn to be in stillness in His presence, silent before Him, for peace to anchor us.

A popular scripture is Psalm 46:10, "Be still, and know that I am God" (NIV), yet many of us do not understand the depth of this scripture. Recognize that in our stillness, as we marinate in His presence, allowing His peace to penetrate our hearts and surpass our restlessness, we experience His truth becoming alive within us. His stillness silences the deafening storm, opening the ears of our understanding. Let's take a closer look at what it means to "be still."

There are two words I would like to concentrate on that are roots for "still." The first is from the Greek word *phimos*, which means "muzzle."[1] In Mark 4:39, we see the word "still" used in this context, "He got up, rebuked the wind, and said to the sea, 'Silence! Be still!' That word muzzle means "to stop" or "subduing to stillness." In that verse in Mark, we can see that Jesus muzzled, subdued, and stopped the storm.

I must touch on this truth of the muzzle. Some may say, "God would never tell us to be quiet," or "He would never put a muzzle on us." Let's agree to disagree because we find stories in Scripture of this very practice. Also, many times, He will ask us or tell us to stop speaking and be silent. God will absolutely subdue us to stillness. Now, why would He even do this? I'll be super honest here. There have been times in my life when God has said, "Maritza, shhhhh," in a very kind way, saying, "Don't say a word." The truth is sometimes, in my frustration, I would say stupid things. These are words that should never have come out of my mouth!

If that isn't enough for you to believe that God would tell us to be silent, let's look at Scripture; read Luke 1:11-20, paying close attention to verse 20.

What do we read? We read in verse 20 that Zechariah was silenced by the Angel Gabriel. In this case, I could absolutely say with no doubt that it sure is possible for the Lord to muzzle us.

In the space below, respond to these questions: Why was Zechariah silenced? And what was it he spoke or said that got him silenced?

We must be careful with what we speak. The Word of God is clear about how there is power in the words we speak. These words create our worlds, and God is so good He would rather us be silent than allow us to speak death over ourselves. Read James 3:1-10 and pay attention to verses 6 and 8. Notice the power the tongue carries. Even Proverbs 18:21 says, "Life and death are in the power of the tongue, and those who

[1] "Phimos," Vine's Complete Expository Dictionary.

love it will eat its fruit." This is why the Lord would sometimes say, "Maritza, stop talking." I was speaking death over my life, which hindered God's blessing of His Word from working within to transform my mind.

It is only when we are in Him that we can truly come to a place of being still and silent to hear what HE has to say and then speak what He says. Find the following scriptures and write them out.

Proverbs 13:3

Proverbs 21:23

Your mouth is what carries power. Pause for a moment and really take an honest look at your own heart. Has the Lord been prompting you to stop speaking? Have you been speaking words that have been bringing death to your life? Be honest with yourself and with God. Repent and start to be still before the Lord.

The only reason He wants us to be still is so we may hear His voice. In hearing His voice, we may hear His plans for us and His instruction. Once we hear His instruction, we are then equipped to only speak what He speaks, which is life-giving. Life in our lives, in our hope, in our family, in our relationships, in our marriages, in our ministries, in our jobs, in our finances and in our future. God truly, truly wants to bless us in a substantial way. He does this when we use His Word with our own mouths.

Dwell in the stillness of silence, the sound of silence—this is where peace resides! To be still, in our silence, is to abide in Him. It is an art; it is a discipline—the discipline of quieting our own thoughts and choosing to listen to His thoughts. I want to share that, as I write this, I have had to walk through trusting God with so much that being still has been the only option I had and continue to have. God asked me to leave my job; mind you, it was my only source of income, and it was a blessed job. Without a doubt, I knew I heard His voice. But honestly, it took me six months to finally say yes to God and two more to leave. And even then, the anxious thoughts started as soon as I left my job. Only by coming into His presence and hearing His voice to get an affirmation of, "Yes, Maritza, you heard correctly," could I get through this season of the unknown. Only in abiding in Him did I get the healing, the guidance, and the peace followed by His ideas.

In the midst of all this, I found myself one day sitting on a rock, looking out at a field of wildflowers, soaking in the sun, watching the field grass flow in the gentle breeze. My mind was suddenly crystal clear as I fully embraced being alive in this glorious moment. I was filled with His peace with glimmers of hope, excitement, and contentment that illuminated my soul, caught up in His peace.

How can I explain this happening? Psalm 46:10 says, "Be still and know." I need to know that I know that I know God has better plans because He loves me, and He will stand by His Word.

It is amazing to see how God then confirms with His Word. That very day, a good friend and brother in Christ who was praying for me sent me a verse in Scripture:

> Consider how the wildflowers grow: They don't labor or spin thread. Yet I tell you not even Solomon in all his splendor was adorned like one of these. If that's how God clothes the grass, which is in the field today and is thrown into the furnace tomorrow. How much more will He do for you—you of little faith? —Luke 12:27-28

It goes on to say in verse 29:

> Don't keep striving for what you should eat and what you should drink, and don't be anxious.

How wonderful it was to see this scripture sent to me right when I had actually "lived out" the verse when I was actually looking and gazing at the field of wildflowers sitting in God's counsel.

God wants us in absolute peace; He knows what we need. Can I tell you how I felt so seen that day, how I indeed felt so at peace knowing God knew what I needed? And this is exactly why I was anxious . . . wondering just how I was going to eat and how I was going to drink when I had no job. God knew. I mean, He is the one who asked me to leave my job. God knows everything about you as well, and He knows what you need in this season and in the future. Be still and know, my friend.

Before you read the rest of this section on peace, I am going to ask you first to think about where in your life you have been unsettled or you have not felt peace. As you go through the rest of this section, bring that to the surface to give to God and let Him work in you to receive the peace you already have in Him.

WHAT IS PEACE?

To really understand what God wants for us and what He has for us, let us look into the word peace! We will dive into this word because as you read, I believe something will unlock in your heart and in your mind to release this peace within you. We want to know what God means when He gives us the peace that is not of this world. Especially that of John 14:27. Look that scripture up and write it below.

One of the definitions for peace found in *Vine's Complete Expository Dictionary* is "free from molestation." Before I move forward on this aspect of peace, I want to acknowledge that when many, including me, hear the word "molestation," we automatically think about sexual molestation or sexual abuse. I do want to take the time to touch on this because, unfortunately, in this broken world, many, both men and women, have been sexually abused in one way or another. So I will say this again: "Free from molestation" is the kind of peace Jesus has for you. If any of you has suffered this kind of abuse, Jesus has come to set you free and heal you so that you may walk in peace. If need be, read it again: "FREE from molestation." Let it sink in, let it seep into your pores, breathe it in, and rest in this truth. "Your faith has healed you. Go in peace and be freed from your suffering" (Mark 5:34 NIV).

The word molestation itself means "to annoy, disturb, or persecute (a person or animal), especially with hostile intent or injurious effect." This is the more precise definition for the word that the *Vines Dictionary* meant when it comes to "free from molestation." I'm going to give the context of some scriptures the *Vines* used for this definition of peace in Luke 11:21 and Acts 9:31.

Luke 11:21 reads: "When a strong man, fully armed, guards his own palace, his goods are in peace" (NKJV). I'm going to start by saying you are a palace. The Holy Spirit chose you to make His home, a dwelling place for the King, a palace. When you realize that you are strong in Him and guard your place in Him, you and all your possessions are at peace; no demon can come and destroy or cause injury in you.

Acts 9:31 says, "So the church throughout all Judea, Galilee, and Samaria had peace, being built up and walking in the fear of the Lord and in the encouragement of the Holy Spirit, and it increased in numbers." You are able to have peace now, being built up and walking in the fear of the Lord and in the encouragement of the Holy Spirit. There is a peace that comes upon you when you know you are walking in Christ, in Him. A peace that comes over you when you walk in the fear of the Lord and not in the fear of man or any other type of fear. Peace knowing who is with you and for you.

In the *New Strong's Concise Dictionary*, we find another word for peace, and that is the word shalom. Shalom means "peace, completeness, welfare, health." But most importantly, "made whole"—nothing missing, nothing broken, made whole. Really think about this one and chew on it. Nothing missing, nothing broken, made whole. For too long, we go through life thinking we are missing so much, missing out, missing material things, missing love, missing peace. I really recommend you look up the following scriptures; I would love to break down each one but will only focus on a few: (Isaiah 26:3 and 34:16, Romans 8:39, James 1:4, Romans 8:32, Job 5:24, Isaiah 40:26, 1 Corinthians 13:12, Hebrews 2:8).

Let us read Isaiah 26:3-13, and, yes, write out verses 3 and 12 below:

Isaiah 26:3

Isaiah 26:12

In this passage of Scripture in Isaiah, we will find much wealth on what it means to be at peace. Sometimes, we need to read Scripture over ourselves out loud because faith comes by hearing. Reading that the Lord is an everlasting rock, we can come to the conclusion that we can stand on Him and that He is a firm foundation that will never be shaken under our feet. It is not like the sand where we are unable to stand firm. We also read in this passage that the path of the righteous He clears and makes straight; if we are in Him, we are righteous, and, therefore, we can stand on this. We are to long for Him in the night and seek Him diligently. And we see that our adversaries, who are the Lord's adversaries, will be put to shame.

Sometimes, we just need to pay more attention to His Word and promises instead of what is happening around us. We are to decree and declare His Word over ourselves and our lives so that we may have this perfect peace from Jesus.

Last, focus on defining peace. Another root word of peace in the Greek is the word *eirene*, which comes from *eiro*, meaning "to join" or "set at one again." In case it has not dawned on you, this book is all about being "in Him," "In Christ Jesus," to be ONE with HIM! When we are one with Him, nothing else matters; all is well. For you to comprehend the love He has for you, look at what Romans 8:38-39 says and hold on to the truth that nothing can separate you from Him—from Him who is love, from Him who is in you!

Take another look at John 14:27 in a different translation: "I leave my peace to you. My own peace I grant to you. I am not granting it to you just like the world grants it. Your heart will never be disturbed and will never fear" (ARTB).

What stands out to you?

Personally, the part that states, "I do not give to you as the world gives," stands out to me. One thing is clear: The peace Jesus has given us is not of this world but one that is perfect in every way.

DO NOT LET YOUR HEART BE TROUBLED

During this season of learning to walk in complete, perfect peace, another song God has brought up is "Good Grace" by Hillsong United, specifically the part of the lyrics that tells us to focus on the Lord and speaks about the heart not being troubled.

This is a truth God wants you to grab hold of—that He does not want your heart to be troubled. Look again at John 14:27 and write down how this verse ends.

God wants pure hearts. Hearts that don't carry the worries or anxieties of the world; He wants to cleanse us of this so we may walk in perfect peace the way He originally created us to walk.

What I have come to realize is when you come to believe without a shadow of a doubt in your mind that you know that you know that God loves you, this truth changes your world. When you keep your eyes on Jesus, on the truth, on love Himself, nothing else really matters. All the things of this world fade away because you are staring at love. When you come to Him and fix your eyes on Him, there is a promise you can take that He will give you peace. Let us look at Philippians 4:6-9. Write it below.

I absolutely can't and won't get over how wonderful Jesus is—to realize He truly exchanges everything that is not good for us with something of His. We are the ones who always get the better part of the deal. He is the God of great and wonderful exchanges, always taking our junk and giving us treasures.

This scripture we just read in Philippians 4 further shows when we come to Him with our requests in prayer, He gives us peace. Once again, we see how we bring our worry through prayer and petition, and with thanksgiving, we make known to Him what we need, what we want, and what it is that we are asking. THEN He gives us peace, the peace of God that surpasses every thought, and it will guard our hearts! Go on, take a breath and breathe in that peace. Once again, in awe—in awe of His goodness for us.

If we keep going to verse 9, we will notice that it gives us a recipe for what we should dwell on so that we may have the God of peace with us all the time. I have to admit that when I am thinking about my needs and going over how to "accomplish them," I have noticed this is when I feel more anxious. But when I focus my thoughts instead on God's ways, peace comes in, and I can live more in the moment. Asking God in prayer for His thoughts and ideas makes a big difference instead of us trying to figure out all the things we can do. Psalm 10:14 says this: "But you, God, see the trouble of the afflicted; you consider their grief and take it in hand. The victims commit themselves to you; you are the helper of the fatherless" (NIV).

Rest assured that God sees your affliction and your grief, He takes it in His hands, and He helps you; He is your helper! Even before you speak a word to Him, before you ask Him and bring your petitions, He sees them. He just wants to pour into you and wants you to approach Him and wants to hear your voice. So go—go to Him and tell Him what you need, casting it all on Him. He is able.

There is a settling in the Spirit for peace to reign in your heart. Look up the following Psalms and write them down.

Psalms 27:3

___

___

Psalm 112:7-8

___

___

Colossians 3:15

___

___

THE PRINCE OF PEACE

Who is the Prince of Peace? This is probably my favorite part of this section and the most important! The Prince of Peace is He who was punished for your peace and died on that cross to give you that peace, Jesus. I have alluded to this a bit, but before I move on, let's read that scripture that tells us about the Prince of Peace.

> For a child will be born for us, a son will be given to us. And the government will be on His shoulders. He will be named Wonderful Counselor, Mighty God, Eternal Father, Prince of Peace. —Isaiah 9:6

Rejoice, rejoice because you have the Prince of Peace. We briefly covered keeping our eyes on Jesus, He who is love! Yet now, let's reach to His other name, Prince of Peace. Recently, I had an experience while on a hike in the Smoky Mountains. I was at a high elevation looking out at the mountain range, taking a deep breath in, and I realized I was at peace. Quickly, God took me to the beaches back in Oregon and California. He had taken me there because He knows I have always told people that the beach is "my happy place" or "the place I go seek peace." As I was standing looking at that view of the mountains, He said, "You have peace at the mountains, at the beach, at your home, and anywhere you go, Maritza. You carry peace; I am in you. You don't have to go anywhere to 'find' peace, Maritza—you already have it; you already possess it in your heart because I am in your heart, the Prince of Peace." That is Jesus, you guys. Jesus lives in me, and I in Him! This is your portion too!!

> Peace I leave with you. My peace I give to you. I do not give to you as the world gives. Your heart must not be troubled or fearful. —John 14:27

Honestly, I don't think we could ever get tired of reading that scripture, or at least we shouldn't get tired of it. This scripture holds so much substance; it is gold. He gives to us peace not as this world gives, but a heavenly peace; the Son of God came down from heaven as flesh with the name Prince of Peace. Peace Himself came down from heaven for you and me, a peace that never ends, that endures forever. Even Ephesians 2:14 tells us that HE is our peace. Praise be to Jesus forever and ever.

> I have told you these things so that in Me you may have peace. You will have suffering in this world. Be courageous! I have conquered the world. —John 16:33

PRAYER

Lord, I am not in a hurry; help my mind to quiet and my heart to not be troubled. I am learning to trust you wholeheartedly; let the peace that you give reign in my heart. Let that same peace that surpasses all understanding flood my mind, and may you, the Prince of Peace, reign and rule over my life all the days of my life. Amen.

CHAPTER 4

JOY IN HIM

You reveal the path of life to me: in Your presence is abundant joy: in Your right hand are eternal pleasures. —Psalm 16:11

This next gift that we are about to dive into is one that I am passionate about. It is so vital for the believer; I would consider it as important as love. It literally gives life to our spirit, to our soul, and to our bones. It will radiate a room and change the atmosphere. It is also a huge spiritual weapon against the enemy. It is one of the fruits of Holy Spirit. It is what defeats depression and the enemy. We are speaking about joy.

The reason I am eager to share is because joy is what the enemy went after in my life, and I even allowed him to take it. I am telling you without joy, it is as if everything we do has no point. This is why I believe joy is as important as love. Joy energizes and ignites; it is like an electric jolt of current, a life-giving current. I imagine it being like the electric current in a defibrillator that makes your heart beat again.

I know there are many in this world who are missing joy, unfortunately even in the church, but this shouldn't be because joy is not an emotion—happiness is. There has been confusion in our society, making them one and the same, but they are not. This is why we will look more at what Scripture tells us about joy, which, by the way, is something that we already possess and is on the inside of us. Joy is not based on circumstances; it is from an internal substance. Happiness is based on what happens to us. Especially as Jesus followers, it is time for us to live in the joy that is for us and not in the despair that the world tells us about.

JOY IN YOU

Restore the joy of Your salvation to me, and give me a willing spirit.
—Psalm 51:12

As we continue this section on joy, I claim this as a prayer unto the Lord for you. May He RESTORE that joy of your salvation. For joy to come back into your life, for it to become real again, all the black and gray in your life is restored with color; all that tried to hinder your joy and tell you that you shouldn't be joyful is removed. All the wonder is restored, that you may have the willing spirit to move past all the disappointment and come into the light and life of true joy.

I want you to notice the word *restore*. Merriam-Webster defines it as "to bring back to or put back into a former or original state." I want to emphasize the description. God restores or brings back to the original state the joy of your salvation. Meaning you have the joy already, and it is being restored.

The journey of the words in these pages is really all about coming back to the place we were with God in the garden, full of Him. That is what having joy restored is all about—living our lives now on earth as it is in heaven.

So let's go! Now that we know this joy is already in us let us comprehend what joy we already carry.

Joy is already in you. It is the joy of His salvation!

JOY IN THE JOURNEY

I'm going to pose the following question to you:

Can you have joy in times of grief?

While writing this, I have literally been on a journey I never planned on—a journey across the country of the United States of America, a journey not knowing where my end destination would be. I'll admit it has been extremely hard and frustrating for me because I have always been a planner. I was always one to calculate time and needed to know where to go and how long. At one of the wonderful homes I had the privilege to stay in, the bathroom had a frame that read: "Find the joy in the journey." Can I tell you how many times I stood in that bathroom just staring at that quote? I gazed, read, and pondered on that quote over and over for about seven days. I would joke that I almost took my coffee and a chair to sit before this quote. It took over a week for me to finally understand what this quote was saying.

The owner of the home is one who helped me see this, a widow of a year who is overflowing with joy. As I admired her ability to walk in joy and learned from her, something two people said to me popped into my mind. The first was from a mentor who I heard say, "Some of you are so focused on the prayer request that has not yet been answered that you are forgetting to be thankful for all the other fruit God has given you." Then the other person, an aunt of mine who walked through stage three cancer and overcame, told me one day as I was out walking with her, "Maritza, you have to learn to stop and smell the flowers."

How many times do many of us walk from point A to point B and miss out on the flowers? Some of us don't even notice them, and others just glance and keep on walking. What my auntie was saying was to stop and admire and smell the fragrance this flower exudes. God wants us to engage in life, engage the senses, and not just pass by the beauty. This is what it comes down to, to enJOY creation, enJOY life, and enJOY the blessings that are in our journey.

I'll admit that this made me realize just how caught up I was in the disappointment of not having what I have wanted since I can remember—the disappointment of feeling rejected. I would get discouraged when I saw others get what *I* wanted and have all their dreams come to fruition. I was so focused on the one request I had asked the Lord, what I had not yet received, and what I was missing, which caused so much grief and despair. When I finally understood that and decided to look at my path—to look at what other blessings I had—that is when I noticed the places I missed out on the joy. I will use this as an example. When I wrote my first book, I didn't get to celebrate in the fullness of that accomplishment. When I went on my first mission trip abroad, I didn't get to enjoy it to the capacity I could have. I was in the middle of being blessed, in the middle of the fruit I missed enjoying fully because, deep down, I was still focusing on what I still lacked per my own expectations.

Have you been overlooking the joy in the journey? Have you, too, walked past the flowers, not taking the time to appreciate and enjoy them? Has God been trying to get your attention, telling you to acknowledge the blessings and the fruit around you? If so, take the time now to write down some of the blessings in your life, even those you can look back on and say, "That is one blessing there I can be thankful for."

As I look back on some blessings I did not appreciate at the time, God, I am thankful and grateful for the following:

The beautiful African sunset I got to see. My first published book. For the stillness of time resting at the property in Tennessee and Kentucky. For the toasted marshmallows. I am grateful for the friends and family who truly care about me and encourage me in the times I need it most.

Your turn—thank God for the blessings you can see in the journey:

Before we move forward, I want to recommend that you take time to ask God to reveal the "little things" that bring you joy. Notice how what you and I wrote are the "little things" that make up life, the daily everyday life events. Finding what brings joy in the little things is really what makes the big difference. Throughout life, I have heard that the activity you can do and actually lose track of time is the thing that fills you with joy. For me, I struggled to find that joy-filled activity. Recently, I learned I absolutely love dancing. When I crank the music up and dance and sing my heart out, it energizes me; it gives me life. Baking is another. I love baking. I love having my morning cup of coffee, I enjoy toasted marshmallows, and I love coloring and painting. It is through such things and activities that we may learn to find joy in the journey. Find what enlivens you, and do more of that. It is in this joy we glorify God and do everything unto Him when we enjoy life.

JOY IS YOUR STRENGTH

Hebrews 12:2 shows the joy set before Him: "Keeping our eyes on Jesus, the source and perfecter of our faith, who for the joy that lay before Him endured a cross and despised the shame and has sat down at the right hand of God's throne."

This is an amazing revelation the Lord shared about how joy gives us strength. First, look up what Nehemiah 8:10 says. Notice what it says about joy: "The joy of the Lord is your strength" (NKJV). Next, look again at what Hebrews 12:2 says, paying attention to what it says about joy: "Keeping our eyes on Jesus, the source and perfecter of our faith, who for the joy that lay before Him endured a cross and despised the shame and has sat down at the right hand of God's throne."

Let's unpack this now. What gave Jesus the strength to go to the cross and endure the pain and suffering was the joy that was set before Him. That joy, if you have not realized this yet, was you. YES, YOU! The joy to see you be with Him and sit with Him in heavenly places, in Him! WOW.

Okay, now that this revelation is in your mind, read what this means for you. That same strength Jesus got while He was praying at the Garden of Gethsemane, asking the Father to take the cup away, is the same strength that now belongs to you as a new creation. The strength came to Him to get up and go be crucified for you and me. Yes, the very same strength is bestowed upon you as you keep your eyes on Jesus.

It is part of that beautiful exchange we made with Him when we decided to crucify our lives with His, as Galatians 2:20 says, and be in Him. That same joy is rightfully ours.

So now what happens is, wherever you are—whether in your bedroom, your living room, your kitchen, your office, at a park—and you are asking God for strength to help you move through whatever you need to get through, all you need to do is see Jesus with arms wide open in front of you, the joy set before you—Him. This is your joy—roles reversed now.

This is our strength—the joy of Jesus, our Lord, is our strength.

WHY ARE YOU CRYING?

> "Weeping may spend the night, but there is joy in the morning."
> —Psalm 30:5

God's magnitude of blessing for us is beyond words. Keeping in mind the joy set before Him gave Him strength to endure, which is for us, we will see how much more He does for us. Yes, the ultimate joy is the joy of being in His presence, the joy of salvation, and the joy of being loved by Him. I am also reminded He blesses us in the midst of grief and sorrow, yet as the God who goes above and beyond what we ask for, He is one to turn it all into joy as we remain and trust in Him.

Let's take a look at a few passages of Scripture:

Luke 7:12–15

John 20:11–18

John 16:20–24

Honestly, I wish I could be right there with you in these verses. I am so amazed at how God speaks, and my desire is that you are also seeing the kindness of the Lord and the joy that is coming to you. Let's start with the passage of Luke 7:12; we see Jesus arrive at the scene as a widow is carrying the dead body of her only son. Scripture says that when Jesus saw this, He had compassion on her; some translations say, "His heart broke," saying, "Don't cry." We read that Jesus told the dead man to arise. The now-living man is presented to his mother alive. Scripture doesn't tell us Mom's reaction, but I could bet that she rejoiced.

Now, let's take a look at the passage of John 20. We start with reading that Mary is standing outside the tomb crying. She looks in the tomb, and we find that two angels ask Mary, "Why are you crying?" After her response, Jesus is the one now standing there, but Mary doesn't recognize Him. Then Jesus asks, "Woman, why are you crying?" She answers Him, and then the next thing out of Jesus' mouth is this one word: "Mary." Again, it doesn't tell us Mary's response, but we do know she says, "Rabbouni!" (Teacher). Looking at Scripture, there is an exclamation point with her response. This exclamation point tells us that Mary was filled with strong emotion. I have a friend who was an English teacher, so I asked, and she confirmed that an exclamation point is used in writing to show the emotions of a character to express strong feelings. I'd like to suggest that what came over Mary was a strong feeling of joy to see her teacher ALIVE. The next verse then says that Jesus had to tell her to not cling to Him. The picture in my mind when I read this is that of Mary about to leap into the arms of Jesus, ready to cling to Him and never let go.

What I absolutely love about these two passages is that Jesus walks in both these stories in the midst of sorrow, in the midst of tears. We see how His heart breaks for those He loves. This means you too. Whatever you are going through, in the midst of your sorrow and in the midst of your tears, Jesus walks in, sees you, and His heart breaks for you. He is MOVED. Hear Him ask, "Why are you crying?" Hear Him call out your name.

Though there is sorrow, there are tears, God is faithful to replace it all, including the pain and suffering, with joy. We will see this even in that excerpt of John 16. We may be in labor pains, but the joy of what is birthed will overshadow the pain in such a way that we will not even remember it.

He promises our grief and sorrow will turn to joy. May we trust and believe the promise keeper in this hour.

THE OIL OF JOY!

Look up Isaiah 61:3 and write it below:

What is so beautiful about this verse is, again, we see the exchange. I am not sure which translation or version of the Bible you used, but other translations translate "oil of joy" as oil of bliss, festive oil, oil of gladness, and oil of merriment.

Just as we discover there is a joy that comes from the labor pains of birthing, there is also pain involved for us to see joy come to fruition in our very own lives as we birth the promises of God over our lives. Many people desire the oil of joy but just want the joy without going through the journey that involves pain. The interesting thing is that it is all about the journey; it is the journey that brings joy. There really isn't any other way to acquire that joy.

Since we are speaking about oil, I will share a bit about this. When I went to Israel a few years back, I got to visit an ancient olive oil processing shop. I learned that the oil is derived by crushing the olive between ginormous stones that grind the olive and drain the oil out. Just like the olive, we, too, need the crushing in our lives in order to get the anointing, the oil, to be released. You have been crushed, pressed, and tested, so that the oil that is within will come out and cover over you.

I will share a few other things about oil, specifically concerning the oil of joy. The root word of oil comes from a word that means "ointment, medicine, perfume and fat." Oil has been a valuable product for centuries, used as a preservative on shield leather, certain furniture, or wood floors that need oil to keep them in good condition. The reason I tell you this is because I want you to understand what this means for you. It means that there is an oil in you, which comes from the crushing—an oil that is coming over you, healing all the wounds and bringing a sweet, fragrant aroma into your life. There is value inside of you, and this oil preserves your life. You will not die in sorrow; you will live in joy.

This makes me think of Mary, who broke the alabaster box to pour it out on Jesus' feet. Something of value had to be broken to release a beautiful aroma. You have been broken, and the oil inside of you is being released. And just as with Mary, when others shamed her and talked negatively about her, Jesus defended her and gave her the honor she deserved for pouring out everything she had for Him and humbling herself before everyone. Jesus gave her the honor of being remembered unto eternity and having her story written in the Holy Bible. Watch as your King honors you, anointing you with oil and setting that banquet table for you before all those who shamed you and wished death upon you. "You prepare a table before me in the presence of my enemies; You anoint my head with oil; my cup overflows" (Psalm 23:5).

RELEASE THE SOUND

I have always admired those who can play instruments. I am mesmerized by music, the sound of the piano and guitars, violin and cellos, and even the accordion and trumpets. When played correctly, all these instruments release the sound they were created to release. We ourselves are instruments of the King. We have been created to release a unique sound with a unique frequency from heaven. God is the One who will blow a fresh wind in us. He is the ultimate musician, and when He touches our heartstrings, we release the sound of joy—the joy of being known, the joy of salvation, and the joy of love. These are some of the sounds of heaven, which we are to release on this earth so we may shift the atmosphere. We carry heaven, and that is exactly what we are to release in this hour—heaven on earth.

Look up the following scriptures and, next to them, describe a sound that you "hear" in the verse.

Revelation 4:8-11 ____________________

Psalm 2:4 ____________________

Luke 15:10 ____________________

Reading these verses, I realize that in heaven, we only hear the sound of reverence where angels say, "Holy, Holy, Holy," giving thanks and the sound of joy and celebration of rejoicing. We even hear God Himself laughing as He sits on the throne! Don't tell me that God is not fun. He actually laughs! This is my desire—to hear His laughter.

That is the same laughter we should carry, one that is straight from the throne room onto this earth. I want to pause and take a moment to express the importance of laughing. I feel that some of you reading this need to learn to laugh again. We often hear a saying that laughter is good medicine. And that is the reason why we need to learn how to laugh, that we may become lighthearted again and no longer carry heavy, broken hearts—to learn to play more and not take ourselves too seriously. I have been guilty of this. Laughter is to fill our lungs again and be released around us, filling the winds of our environment with it. When we take it further, that laughter, that sound of heaven, is one that the devil cannot take. He can't stand it. If he can't stand it, why are we not laughing more, rejoicing more, and dancing more?

Today, I had the privilege to go to a friend's house and pray over her home and her children's room. We started praying in the Spirit, then in English, and then we started thanking and praising with clapping our hands. We finished with a dance party to a joyful song. Can I tell you that the atmosphere of that home shifted dramatically, the sound of heaven came, and peace settled.

I am reminded of a song by Rend Collective, "Hallelujah Anyway." This song speaks about praising the King even through a broken heart. This makes me think just how worthy God is of our praise. We can praise Him just because He loves us. That is all we need: His love—the love of the Great I Am. Let me even share that one time, as I was in worship, my eyes full of tears, I felt like Hannah. The words coming out of my mouth were, "You are worthy of it all, Lord." I recall God asking me, "Maritza, if I am worthy of it all, am I not worthy of your dancing too, not just your tears?" This was a shift for me in understanding how praising Him with joy because of who He is changes the focus to Him.

As we praise, our own hearts change, and we release joy in our surroundings. My favorite insight is realizing that just like Shadrach, Meshach, and Abednego all said they would not bow down to an idol "even if" the Lord didn't rescue them. When I remember this story, I also remember that the Lord did indeed rescue them. This means that if we have an "even if" moment, we can praise Him because the *even if* means He will, and He already has; it may not look like we think, yet He already has. So no matter the circumstances, it is time to release the sound of joy. It is our joy and praise that will bring change to our circumstances.

Again, remember: Our bodies have vocal cords; we have heartstrings just like stringed instruments. We can clap our hands, and a sound is made that creates a joyful sound. You are an instrument of God, created to bring the sound of heaven. Your heavenly sound matters.

May our hearts praise Him, and may we sing to Him because He is our strength and shield (Psalm 28:7); may we remember how exactly He brought His people out, with rejoicing and shouts of joy. It is in remembering who He is and what He has done for us, but most importantly, in the very fact that we belong to Him that will spring up shouts of joy. It is in coming back to Him, to His presence, that we find our joy again. Psalm 16:11 declares: "You reveal the path of life to me; in Your presence is abundant joy; in Your right hand are eternal pleasures." It is in the laughter, in the oil, in the strength that we get back into His presence in that Garden, in His throne room, where we find that joy again. Or I should say instead that the joy is restored just as He originally gave to us.

Keep on dancing, for you belong to Him. "Always be joyful because you belong to the Lord. I will say it again. Be joyful" Philippians 4:4 (NIRV).

PRAYER

Jesus, I thank you for the pressing. I thank you for coming into my life during a time of sorrow and tears. I will let the oil of joy be released; I will let the sound of joy, the sound of laughter, come out of my inner being. I thank you that you have given me the oil of joy, the garment of praise, and beauty from ashes. Amen.

CHAPTER 5

RIGHTEOUS IN HIM

That is, God's righteousness through faith in Jesus Christ, to all who believe, since there is no distinction. —Romans 3:22

It is a wonder to think about all the spiritual gifts God freely gives us. How beautiful it is that our magnificent God would give us the inheritance of the kingdom of heaven—an inheritance like no other, and all we must do is believe, truly believe. Also, we must keep in mind that not everyone gets this inheritance. Not everyone gets to live a life in the fullness that Jesus came to give; not everyone gets to live that life of power and authority.

Some may get upset at the following statement, but there are even some professing Christians who are not inheriting the kingdom of God. It is only the children of God who get His inheritance. If you call yourself a Christian and you are reading this and getting irritated, I want you to know I am not saying this to condemn. Absolutely not! I bring this up so if you truly want to partake of this inheritance, I give you the opportunity to let the light come in and to give you the time to repent. Scripture is so clear about the inheritance being for the righteous.

I want to solidify with what Scripture tells us of who will not inherit the kingdom. Look up and read 1 Corinthians 6:9–10 and list what these verses say of who will not inherit God's kingdom.

Again, this is a time for reflection. I'm going to say this: The inheritance, full inheritance, is amazing to have, yet the ultimate inheritance is having the love of God, who is love.

If you wrote the characteristics of those who won't inherit the kingdom of God, and you relate to one of them now, more than likely, it is due to a hurt or trauma from your past that has caused you to harden your heart and not let love in. This world only offers false, temporary pleasures that only give the illusion of being loved or happy. Friend, nothing else will do besides the love of He who is love, Christ Jesus. If we go further in that scripture, it reads as follows: "And some of you used to be like this. But you were washed, you were sanctified, you were justified in the name of the Lord Jesus Christ and by the Spirit of our God" (1 Corinthians 6:11).

Before we dig deeper into being righteous in Him, I want to share this next scripture so you may know God's vast kindness. I want you to receive His kindness and believe the words that when you are in Him and repent and confess with your mouth, He is truly faithful and righteous to forgive you and to cleanse you from ALL unrighteousness. You can find this truth in 1 John 1:9. Find it, write it below, and write what it means for you:

> Or do you despise the riches of His kindness, restraint, and patience, not recognizing that God's kindness is intended to lead you to repentance?
> —Romans 2:4

Repentance and confessing are key to removing all unrighteousness to receive His righteousness.

BLOOD THAT PURIFIES

So what does it really mean to be righteous? I do want to touch a bit on this because it will help you understand what it is that God has done. While digging deeper into this word, I learned that "righteous" in Hebrew stems from a word that is a legal term, *tsadaq*, which means to be "justified and cleared of all charges." Before we go any further, I want you to see how none of us are righteous except for Him, Christ Jesus. Read Romans 3:9–20 and then Revelation 5:1–10.

In the space provided below, write how this passage in Romans explains our condition.

Now, in Revelation, write why John started to cry, and then write what the elder tells him.

I had you look at these excerpts of Scripture because it is clear that none of us were righteous, none of us were worthy to open this scroll, all of us have sinned, and all of us have been stained. Only One was found worthy to open the scrolls, only One is righteous, and that One is Jesus. Yet Jesus didn't want us to go to hell, and this is where we encounter His kindness and goodness. He died so that we may be righteous *in Him*. Ephesians 1:7 tells us, "We have redemption in Him through His blood, the forgiveness of our trespasses, according to the riches of His grace." When Jesus died on the cross, He cleared our debts. With His blood, He washed our wickedness away and claimed us as free of wrong. In essence, to be declared righteous with the righteousness of God is the pronouncement of innocence.

Search out the following verses and write them below:

Romans 5:8-9

In the chapter "Beginning in Him," I talked about the blood and how Jesus' blood was declared innocent by Pilate. We can be confident that the blood of Jesus is what has declared us as righteous; it is what has cleansed us, and it is only because of His blood that we are justified in the courts of heaven, in which our Judge, our God, can see us without sin. It is all because of what Jesus did; we cannot save ourselves, and there is nothing we can ever do to try to justify ourselves, to try to make ourselves right before Him. It is only by accepting what Jesus did and believing in His blood that we can walk rightly before God and others with all humility.

I love how the book of Romans shares the difference between the law and the Spirit. As we learned earlier in this chapter, righteous is a term used in the process of justice—to be justified. Rules go only so far, but they don't cleanse us; they instead remind us more and more of our shortcomings, bringing condemnation. Look, I grew up hearing that I had to go to a priest, tell them what sin I committed, and they would give me a ritual to perform in words so many times—which carried no substance and was powerless—that I would be made clean. When I did these acts, they never made me clean or right; inside, I still felt dirty and unworthy. Rules, regulations, and laws will not get you redeemed, cleansed, or righteous. 1 Timothy 1:9–11 is clear that the law was not written for those who are righteous, which, as we are learning, are those who are in Christ and born of the Spirit, the true children of God who by faith received the righteousness in Him.

> We know that the law is not meant for the righteous person, but for the lawless and rebellious, for the ungodly and sinful, for the unholy and irreverent, for those who kill their fathers and mothers, for murderers, for the sexually immoral and homosexuals, for kidnappers, liars, perjurers, and for whatever else is contrary to the sound teaching based on the glorious gospel of the blessed God, which was entrusted to me. —1 Timothy 1:9–11

I have to admit those verses in 1 Timothy sound extremely familiar to the verse in 1 Corinthians, which we referenced to help bring repentance. I tell you: God is serious about His Word. We can take His Word and receive the truth that it is by His blood we are cleansed and live by the Spirit instead of the law because none of us can do anything to justify ourselves. "'Come, let us discuss this,' says the Lord. 'Though your sins are like scarlet, they will be as white as snow; though they are as red as crimson, they will be like wool'" (Isaiah 1:18). WOW! I urge you to perceive that in this verse, there is an invitation—an invitation in which the Lord Himself is calling you to have a conversation with Him to talk to Him and allow Him to speak truth into your life. Will you accept this invitation?

GIFT OF GRACE

There is a huge deception amongst the church, with many believing that because Jesus forgave our sins on the cross, past, present, and future, it is okay to go do whatever one pleases, including blatant sin. I have heard people misinterpret "being under grace" as an excuse to do wicked things, exclaiming, "It is okay because grace covers all actions." Well, I am here to declare the truth: The gift of grace is not to be taken advantage of, and it does not absolve us of our sin when we are consciously and defiantly sinning. This is what the Word of God says: "For if we *deliberately* sin after receiving the knowledge of the truth, there no longer remains a sacrifice for sins, but a terrifying expectation of judgment and the fury of a fire about to consume the adversaries" (Hebrews 10:26–27, emphasis mine). We see here that to deliberately sin after receiving the knowledge of the truth, the truth of Jesus dying for our sins, brings judgment, leaving no other sacrifice for the forgiveness of our sins. In the Message translation, it explains that we are "turning our backs" on Jesus when we sin after learning the truth. The question posed in that translation of the Bible is this: "What do you think will happen if you turn on God's Son, spit on the sacrifice that made you whole, and insult this most gracious Spirit?" I must pause here and let you really ponder that question. The gift of grace is not a reason for you and me to commit deliberate sin!

His grace for salvation is through grace: "You are saved by grace through faith, and this is not from yourselves; it is God's gift" (Ephesians 2:8). Through grace, we were saved, and through grace, we also receive the righteousness, the kindness of God—His kindness for us who have all fallen short of His glory.

Let's look at what Romans 3:22-26 declares; go read that and then write down verses 23 and 24 below.

We find how it is through His grace we are justified and that when we have faith in Him, we are declared righteous. It is through His grace and God's gladness to give us His reflection, declaring us righteous!

Let me share something that goes with us being under grace in Him, which does not mean we can just go sin as we have covered. I want to touch on God's kindness more. Here is Romans 2:4 again: "Or do you despise the riches of His kindness, restraint, and patience, not recognizing that God's kindness is intended to lead you to repentance?" In a study of the fruits of the spirit, one of my mentors explained kindness, one of the fruits of the Spirit, as "like a moral goodness or moral choice." She further explained it as "extending a grace, a knowing offer of love and grace, where there is no condemnation, no malice, no ridicule." Kindness is a focus on others' needs instead of one's own problems; it is, as she further mentioned, "loaning one's strength instead of weakness." As I listened, it dawned on me how this is exactly why kindness is what leads to repentance. This is the fruit that moved Jesus to extend His righteousness unto us, not condemning us, not shaming us, but loving us. He gave us His strength in our weakness of the flesh, gifting us His Spirit full of righteousness and goodness. He extended His grace to us, a selfless, holy, and pure grace.

Search out Romans 8:1-2 and write it down below:

These verses you just wrote carry power and life. When you understand there is no condemnation when you walk in Christ and when you are walking in the Spirit, sin has lost its grip over you.

DECLARED HOLY, PURE, AND BLAMELESS

"Abraham believed God, and it was credited to him for righteousness."
—Romans 4:3

When I read this, I couldn't help but ponder on the words in that verse for a while; all I kept thinking was, "Righteousness only comes by believing." It sounds so simple, yet so hard because we know our own ways, thoughts, and actions, and we think God would never think of us as righteous; there is no way we could ever be holy, pure, and blameless. The beauty of His extension of grace is that when we believe—and mainly when we repent of our own ways—He bestows that righteousness on us.

Let us look at Romans 3:26: "God presented Him to demonstrate His righteousness at the present time, so that He would be righteous and declare righteous the one who has faith in Jesus." With that verse, I am also adding the following verse for you to read: "But now He has reconciled you by His physical body through His death, to present you holy, faultless, and blameless before Him" (Colossians 1:22).

There is something about the word declare. In the verse of Romans we just read, it states He would declare righteous the one who has faith in Jesus. When we look at the scripture in Colossians, we see that with the body of Jesus, you and I have been reconciled and are presented as holy, faultless, and blameless!

Look, this is what it also means to be righteous: to be announced as blameless, pure, and holy by the King of kings and Lord of lords. He is the One who decided He wanted to call you holy. We can see in Isaiah 61 that He Himself wraps us in the robe of righteousness. Can you imagine? He takes our wretched rags stained with the crimson of our sin, and He places His snowy white robe over us. What a King we have, so good and kind, who robes us and declares us pure, holy, and blameless.

I want to give you one more passage of Scripture to show you that Jesus calls you holy and blameless. There is such importance in understanding our right standing in Christ. Believing that we are righteous is what allows us to come boldly to the throne.

Look at Ephesians 5:25-27; write below what it explains Jesus did and why.

As I reread this passage in my Bible translation (HCSB), I saw a word that never jumped at me until now. He wanted to present His bride in splendor! I can only imagine what that holy and blameless looks like, full of splendor. That is what you look like to God when you have believed what Jesus has done for you and wholeheartedly decided to take His righteousness. It is only through faith in His Son that you get there, not works—which never get you right in His sight.

Remember, there is nothing you can do to become righteous; it is a gift. The Word also explains that it is only those with pure hearts and clean hands that get to ascend to the mountain (Psalm 24:4). Again, there is nothing that we can do to get there; we can only come to Jesus with repentance opening our hearts, asking Him to search our hearts and remove any spot or wrinkle as Ephesians describes; through faith we can believe that we are DECLARED pure, holy, and blameless because He already has declared us as such.

BLESSED

Open your spiritual ears and listen here to what the angels and the living creatures, along with the elders in the throne room, say in a loud voice: "The Lamb who was slaughtered is worthy to receive power and riches and wisdom and strength and honor and glory and blessing!" (Revelation 5:12). There are many reasons I bring this part of Scripture up as we discover what righteousness is for us. Did you know that when we are in right standing with God, by being cleansed by the blood of the slaughtered Lamb, it gives us access to the throne room? Let me remind you of this: Jesus gave us His robe of righteousness.

The Lamb is worthy to be given many things; among them is blessing. I share this because I want to show you that though He is the only One who was found worthy, He has given us His righteousness, and we also sit on the throne with Him, co-seated. What I want to connect here is that what He is receiving in this last verse of Revelation is also what we receive, and as we receive blessing, we are called blessed!

I will disclose that in the last few months of this season, there were a few times that I felt like a burden. There were situations and comments that led me to believe this was true and that it was my identity, a burden. BUT GOD! What He says about me is that I am blessed! Look—to God, we are not a burden; He delights in blessing us. I have mentioned before how Ephesians 1:3 is an important verse for understanding what the fullness in Christ is about: "Praise the God and Father of our Lord Jesus Christ, who has BLESSED us in Christ with every spiritual blessing in the heavens" (emphasis mine). This verse tells us we receive spiritual blessings from heaven, blessings that entail the character of Christ, the fruits of the spirit, and gifts of the spirit. To be blessed is the encompassing essence of the heavens, the full substance of Jesus—of which, again, that verse of Revelation 5:12 gives a glimpse. This is who we are in Him, an embodiment of Christ, full of blessing.

Name a few blessings that pop into mind below:

We are blessed with every spiritual blessing I have covered thus far: faith, peace, joy, righteousness, and more to come in the following pages. I urge you to dig into the remaining blessings and even those I didn't get to cover that you may have written down yourself. These all come from heaven.

Though we see Scripture has given us truth about what it means to be blessed, I want to share what I found "blessed" means and why it is important for us. A brief Google search of "blessed definition" describes the word blessed as "made holy and consecrated" and "those who live with God in heaven." What a fitting word for this section of righteous in Christ. To be blessed in a term that the world gives, not just the Bible, means to be holy and consecrated. We can honestly stop here regarding being blessed; however, there is more you must comprehend about the matter.

Hopefully, you are as excited about this as I am because we are speaking about what is given to you, about you being blessed and what this means and looks like. As for what it looks like, let me start with what it does not look like! It does not look like one who walks around in worry, shame, or anxiety. It does not look like poverty, and it does not look like scraps. I will cover a few things about the inheritance we have in Christ in the next part of what we have in Him. What I want you to understand is what is written in Deuteronomy Chapter 28, verses 1 through 14. Go read this for yourself and see just how much God wants to bless you for being righteous in Him and obeying His Word.

In this area, write down all the blessings that God speaks of in those verses:

Now that you have that written out, grasp that these are the blessings God has for you. Look, being blessed is not about having all the riches in the world; it is about having all the riches in glory in Christ Jesus. The riches in heaven. Yet, we are to REFLECT His glory, His blessing, His abundance that He gives us from heaven onto this earthly realm. If there is abundance in Christ, we are to reflect this on this earth. Being blessed is to have the favor of the Lord; it is to radiate His goodness and shine so bright in joy.

I have no proof of this idea at the moment, but I feel I need to share it with you. I envision joy has a frequency of light. The more joy we have, the more we radiate like the sun. I want to give you a few more scriptures. "The righteous thrive like a palm tree and grow like a cedar tree in Lebanon" (Psalm 92:12). In this verse, we see that the righteous are to thrive, not just try to survive or hardly make it or fail. No! We are to thrive, we are to prosper as our soul prospers, and we are to be blessed and be a blessing to this world! How else are people going to see the goodness of God if we, as His children, as His chosen ones, don't walk in that fullness Jesus came to give, called abundance? Allow me to have you go look up one more verse on this, Psalm 5:12, and write it out below.

Can we get a "glory hallelujah"? Seriously! All this is done just by having faith in Jesus! He came to give us His righteousness, removing the duty of the law and showing us His love through kindness that leads us to repentance, then leads us to become righteous in Him and fully blessed. "And be found in Him, not having a righteousness of my own from the law, but one that is through faith in Christ" (Philippians 3:9).

Praise the King of kings for the faith He has given us, that we may be found in Him, holy and righteous.

PRAYER

Here is my heart, Lord; I ask that you search it for any spot or wrinkle. I allow you to purify my heart through Your blood. I confess that there is nothing I can do to become righteous; I ask for forgiveness for any time I have taken advantage of your gift of grace and repent for it. Today, I choose to believe you have already declared me pure, holy, and blameless and that you want to bless me through your righteousness. Amen.

CHAPTER 6

INHERITANCE IN HIM

I pray that the perception of your mind may be enlightened so you may know what is the hope of His calling, what are the glorious riches of His inheritance among the saints.
—Ephesians 1:18

In a recent dream, I was sitting at an executive table, with people sitting all around with me. I told those at the table, "It is amazing we get the gift of salvation; there is no greater gift, but with this gift comes an inheritance, and I want that inheritance! I want everything that comes with that."

I would like to suggest that if you are reading this, you are at that table with me. You are listening; you are searching. You truly want everything that God has for you. I am not going to deny that the greatest gift God has given us is His love. Because of His great love, He sent His one and only Son to give us eternal life and salvation (John 3:16). Another scripture,1 John 3:1, says, "Look at how great a love the Father has given us that we should be called God's children. And we are!"

Let us pause here for a second. Think about what this means. We are HIS children! Usually, when a parent dies, they leave an inheritance to their kin. Granted, I understand that this has not happened for everyone reading this, which is why I will instead share what Proverbs 13:22 says: "A good man leaves an inheritance to his grandchildren." Well, Jesus did die, and it is written that everything He owns is ours. I hope you heard that—EVERYTHING He owns is ours.

Take the time to read John 16:15 and write it down in the section below:

Okay, just wow—you see, everything that belongs to Jesus and to the Father is also ours. It is our inheritance for those who believe. Specifically also for those who are in Him. This is a hard concept for people to comprehend, but when you really ponder about this, God created everything seen and unseen. We have the power and dominion over these, but too many people are living a life not believing the truth we just wrote from John 16:15. A harder concept to conceive is the ownership in the unseen. We have storehouses in heaven, and we are citizens of heaven; therefore, we have access to these storehouses even as we walk on this earth. We are to draw on what God has already blessed us with, the spiritual gifts.

EXPOSE AND BREAK

During this time of writing, God brought to my attention the following in regard to our inheritance: the exposure of what keeps us from stepping into the manifestation of our inheritance, of us walking fully and confidently in it. That something is the poverty mindset. Allow me to clarify. It is where the mind has set its beliefs, where it has made up its "mind" on a subject consciously or unconsciously. To take this further, the mind makes up part of our soul. What is in the mind is etched in our soul, whether we know it or not. Erick Erikson's theory in psychosocial development tells us that the will is developed by the age of three.[2] Bring in all the worldly spiritual strongholds—even generational ones in human blood, which, by the way, blood speaks—and these strongholds, what is in our soul, mind, will, and emotions, hold us back from walking fully in what Jesus has given us at the cross.

I'm going to share a few things, and I ask that you come along with me. Ask yourself if any of this is highlighted for you.

First, as I mentioned earlier in the book, God asked me to leave my job with no next job in sight or anything lined up. Well, what transpired very shortly after was that God exposed the altar of money in my soul, which was mainly on my mind. The altar of money exposed! Be ready for this. How do we know if we still have an altar and idolize money? Here it is. Ask yourself this question: "How much time do I spend every day thinking about my financial life—my income, bills, past and upcoming purchases, and investments?" in comparison to how much time you spend meditating upon God's

[2] Saul Mcleod, PhD, "Erik Erikson's Stages of Psychosocial Development," Simple Psychology, October 16, 2023. https://www.simplypsychology.org/erik-erikson.html.

Word. With this, He revealed the poverty spirit and mindset that followed me from generations past.

Be serious, take the time now, and pay attention without any condemnation.

You see when the question was posed to me, I realized at that very moment I still had an altar for money where I was worshiping it. My mind and my thoughts were on how I would make money and pay bills. Money was on my mind more than God or His Word. Altar and idol exposed!

So what breaks this? We get a brief insight within the question posed in order to expose the altar. It asked, "In comparison to meditating upon God's Word." Start meditating on God's Word to renew your mind and start thinking the way God thinks. Find Philippians 4:8 and write that down in the space provided.

My Bible translation says *dwell*. Dwell on these things. We are to start setting our minds on the things above, on Jesus. I have more to share in a later chapter on this word dwell.

Now, let me expose that spirit of fear. The poverty mindset works very close with the spirit of fear—the fear that there won't be enough, the fear of lack. Those are removed as we dwell on He who is our great provider. But I want to focus a bit on the generational strongholds here.

First, I acknowledge that some of you may think, "But when I received Jesus, I became a new creation, and all the generational things are done." Well, for our spirit, yes. But again, our blood has to be washed and replaced with the blood of Christ. Scripture mentions that our blood speaks and cries out to God. Read Genesis 4:10, and write it below:

Okay, so Abel's blood cried out; it spoke of what happened. Events, hurt, betrayal . . . God hears it. Poverty in our blood from past sins of our ancestors? Jesus breaks and cleanses it with HIS BLOOD!

Write out Matthew 26:28.

Maritza, I don't understand. If Jesus cleansed me, then why is this still lingering? Well, the best way to say it is that, out of trauma, our soul fragments—again, the soul is the mind, will, and emotions. Faith comes by hearing. For so long, we may hear that we don't have enough. Our fear speaks louder than our belief in what Jesus did because we have lived in the lies of the world too long. We NEED to grasp the mind of Christ and the new creation fully to really be able to receive the full inheritance. This is where communion with God is essential for our life in Christ—not only the communion of the blood and the body with the elements but also the communion of spending time with God and dwelling in Him, on Him, and with Him.

Another quick story. As I was getting ready to leave on a mission trip abroad, I was talking to someone who was telling me that I didn't need to go so far away—that I could stay local and help people here. This person then proceeded to tell me a bit about their past. On my drive home, I had a conversation with God because I started feeling doubt creeping in after having the conversation with that person. How did God respond? "For My thoughts are not your thoughts, and your ways are not My ways" (Isaiah 55:8). Right after that: "Maritza, that person was speaking from their own experience and understanding, which came from a spirit of fear and lack. You, on the other hand, hear and heed My voice."

Look up Proverbs 3:5 and write it out!

Now look at 3:6 and write it below.

Many of us know verse 5, but we tend to stop there and not read verse 6. Yes, He will direct our paths, but only by doing the command at the beginning of this verse: THINK about Him. Depending on the translation of your Bible, you may find the words *acknowledge, submit,* or *know* Him.

That scripture is KEY to this life in Christ, the life to the fullest with all the spiritual blessings He has already given us. We must trust God with all our hearts and minds, not lean on our own understanding, because His ways are higher and better than what we can ask, think, or imagine.

Trust the Lord with all your heart, and do not lean on your own understanding.

Stop partnering with the poverty mindset.

Let me be transparent here: Some of us keep partnering with that poverty mindset when God is telling us, "I have the best!" Though God spoke to me and exposed this, He showed me I needed to stop partnering with the poverty mindset. If you haven't figured it out yet, the spirit realm is real, and what we agree upon and partner with can have a hold on us and keep us from our full potential.

Storytime: I needed new jeans. Keep in mind I have no job, and so, yeah, money was on my mind. Exposed! I was at a cute boutique looking at the jeans, and the person I was with mentioned there was a thrift shop a couple doors down. I put the jeans back on the shelf and walked over to the thrift shop. I made a purchase. As soon as I walked out the door, I heard in such a kind and loving, yet stern, voice, "Maritza, why did you partner with that?" Exposed again! I promise you—I fought the tears from rolling down my cheeks. Jesus continued: "You are My Bride, and I have the best of the best for you. I don't have used-up rags for you; I have only royal garments."

That is exactly what Jesus is telling you now! He is saying to you, "Stop partnering with poverty and walk in faith, knowing that I have the best for you."

Expose and break in the mighty blessed name of Jesus.

1. What does your mind think about most?

2. Have you been partnering with poverty and fear of not having enough, and God is asking you to stop?

THE BANQUET TABLE

Many have lived in a place of scarcity with the poverty mindset—where we have focused far too long on the next meal, worried about how we will get the next meal, and even living "paycheck to paycheck."

God already has a banquet table ready for us, FULL of all that we need. The riches in glory, the bread, the wine, the milk and honey, and then some. Come and take your place; take your seat at the banquet table where the goods never cease.

> And wine that makes glad the heart of man, oil to make his face shine, and bread which strengthens man's heart. —Psalm 104:15 NKJV

My friend, understand that there is a seat already there for you. If you are waiting for an invitation, here it is: come to the table, take a seat. Jesus has already prepared this table, and even better, Scripture says He prepared it in the presence of our enemies. Sit confidently, owning that seat, owning your place at the table, eating of the goodness of the Lord and ENJOYING His presence and gift to you.

Read and write Psalms 23:5-6 below:

AN INHERITANCE FOR THE RIGHTEOUS

> A good man leaves an inheritance to his grandchildren, but the sinner's wealth is stored up for the righteous. —Proverbs 13:22

It is amazing to think God loves His children so much—those who follow His decrees, calling them righteous. He cares so much He would take the wealth of the wicked to give to the righteous. This blows my mind. I have to say that this is no excuse for a child of God to be lazy and sit and do nothing and wait for wealth to come to them. No. If you follow Jesus, you know that there is much work to be done. The work of the kingdom of God is different. Yet some He also gives talents, gifts, and skills to use on this earth to build wealth. With that said, I am not giving you permission to just stop working and sit around and do nothing and wait for wealth. BUT if God calls you to leave your job to do His kingdom works, then rest assured that He will use even the wealth of the wicked to help you with building His kingdom. For those of you needing scripture for this reality, here we go: Psalm 135:10-12 says, "He struck down many nations and slaughtered mighty kings: Sihon king of the Amorites, Og king of Bashan, and all the kings of Canaan. He gave their land as an inheritance, an inheritance to His people Israel." Here, we see a psalm praising Yahweh for having dispossessed kings by slaughtering them and giving their land to His people. We can also witness this in Deuteronomy 6, verses 10 through 11. "When the Lord your God brings you into the land He swore to your fathers Abraham, Isaac, and Jacob that He would give you—a land with large and beautiful cities that you did not build, houses full of every good thing that you did not fill them with, wells dug that you did not dig, and vineyards and olive groves that you did not plant—and when you eat and are satisfied." Look, I have to admit this makes me joyful. God is the God who gives and takes away. We must learn to be grateful in all seasons. Get back into your Bible and look up what verse 12 says, which finishes the sentence that began in verse 11, "When you eat and are satisfied."

What does that verse tell us we must do when we eat and are satisfied?

We must not forget our Lord Jesus Christ—the God who has brought us out of our slavery mindsets of this world and brought us into His glorious riches in glory. Hallelujah!

AN INHERITANCE THROUGH OBEDIENCE

Obedience—a word that comes with conviction. I believe this is not just me, but I sometimes feel like this word has a negative undertone that comes with it. As if it's an "I have to do" task where you begrudgingly do the things asked. What many don't understand is how true obedience will come when we decide that we love God and blessings come from obedience. John 14:15 says, "If you love me, you will keep My commands." If you take notice, you will realize that when you love someone, you WANT to do anything for them. It isn't forced; it comes from the heart. I pray this is the kind of obedience you get to.

We recently read Deuteronomy 6:10-12. Those verses start under the subtitle "Remembering God through Obedience" in my personal Bible. The beautiful epiphany here is it shows that obedience is a way to show someone you love that you love them. It also makes me think when you love someone, you constantly think of them or constantly remember them. The Lord wants us to remember Him and His goodness. It is through obedience—because we love—that gifts and blessings follow.

MARVELOUS STORIES OF INHERITANCE

Let us look at a couple stories straight from the Bible. Let's go to the book of Esther and start with how her story begins in Scripture. Esther 2:7 says, "Mordecai was the legal guardian of his cousin Hadassah (that is, Esther), because she didn't have a father or mother." This is how Esther is introduced; she was an orphan with no mother or father. Since we are in the exposing business, let me quickly expose another thing right now: the orphan mindset. We will soon get back to Esther; this is important for you. You are not alone, not unloved, and not rejected. God has adopted you, calls you son, calls you daughter. He says you are accepted, loved, and you belong. Look up the following scriptures and write them out:

Ephesians 1:4-5

Romans 8:15

Back to Esther. More than likely, you are familiar with her story, but in case you are not, let's refresh. This book begins with King Ahasuerus being married to Queen Vashti, but due to her disobedience to the king, her royal position was to be given to another woman. We learn in Esther 2:17 that Esther is the woman who becomes queen to replace Vashti. She became queen at a crucial time in history when the Israelites were taken into exile, and an evil man named Haman was poisoned with the idea of annihilating the Jews. There is so much wealth in this book, but to get to the point I want to make, I am going to fast-forward to Esther 3:10–13, where we learn there was a decree Haman sent out into all of Persia after the king removed his signet ring and gave it to Haman, giving him full authority to do as he wished.

Now we are at the moment everyone in Christian communities knows this book for, Esther 4:14. Esther is now caught in a moment of having to decide whether to go before the king or not to go before the king. This was a life-and-death decision, a death sentence because, as it says in verse 4:11, anyone who approached the king in the inner courtyard without being summoned by him was to receive the death penalty. As we continue reading, we learn that, indeed, she went before the king unsummoned, her life was spared, and all Jews lived—none died.

To understand the connection between obedience and inheritance, we observe Esther had not been summoned to the king's presence for at least thirty days. Note also that the inner courtyard was the place of intimacy. Esther wasn't only facing a decision; she was staring fear and death in the face with the act of obedience to God to save the Jews.

Notice the king's response to Esther in the following verses and write them out in the space provided:

Esther 5:3 ________________

Esther 5:6 ________________

Esther 7:2 ________________

"Up to half the kingdom." Not only did the king say this to Esther once, but THREE times!! Because of her obedience. The king's response was, "ASK and up to half the kingdom I give to you." Can we get a hint here?! The earthly king would give Esther up to half the kingdom because he loved her so much. How much more will our heavenly King of kings give us? The thing is, He already has. He already gave us the whole kingdom of heaven.

If Esther's story isn't enough, let us now see the story of Jehu.

Who is Jehu? Turn to 2 Kings and go to chapter 9, verses 2 through 5. We learn that Jehu is a commander of the army of Ahab's sons and, at one point, rode with Ahab himself. In the verses provided, we see he has been anointed as king over Israel. As we read this chapter, we read that when Jehu was anointed king, he was given a command: "You are to strike down the house of your master Ahab" (2 Kings 9:7). I don't know about you, but as I read "strike down the house of your master," you better know that you know; either you are all in or don't try anything at all. Praise God Jehu was a soldier, and he knew the command came from someone higher than his master on earth. Indeed, Jehu strikes down the house of Ahab, killing all his sons—all seventy. He also sets out to take care of Jezebel with all her witchcraft and even the prophets of Baal. Indeed, Jehu obeyed. Because of his obedience, he inherited the land and the people.

In both these stories, note that first, Esther was already in the position of queen, and second, Jehu was already anointed as king, BUT they both had to act on obedience in order to fully possess their inheritance. Some of you reading this have already been anointed, and God has already given you instruction. It is now up to you to make the move, to step out in obedience to fully possess your inheritance.

UTMOST INHERITANCE

By now, we see we have an amazing gift, but wait—there is more! This is our God, the God of more—more than we ask, think, or imagine! There is an inheritance that is beyond what we comprehend currently, but it is clear in Scripture; once we grasp it, it is the utmost beautiful inheritance besides Jesus Himself. This inheritance has been given to us right from the beginning, an inheritance given to us before the foundation of the world. We will be planting ourselves spiritually in Genesis, and we will grow there until eternity. Read Genesis 1:1-3.

That last verse says, "Then God said, 'Let there be light,' and there was light." There is so much substance in this right now. I feel it, and I sure hope you do too. "'Let there be light,' and there was light." Do you realize the power we are reading about currently? In an earlier section, I mentioned the power of our words. God spoke, and when He spoke, what He spoke manifested. He created what He spoke; He created light.

Now go to Ephesians 1:18 in the Passion Translation and write it out below.

We will continue in Ephesians. Read Ephesians 1:19-22 and then Ephesians 2:6. As we read, we will see that we have been raised with Jesus into the heavenly realm, co-seated with Jesus. Now, we, too, have the ability and the power to create. Look, God has given us the inheritance of the power to create IN HIM. Just as God spoke to create, so can we.

> I pray that the light of God will illuminate the eyes of your imagination flooding you with light, until you experience the full revelation of the hope of his calling—that is, the wealth of God's glorious inheritances that he finds in us, his holy ones. —Ephesians 1:18 TPT

In this scripture, we see Paul pray that the eyes of our imaginations would be illuminated by His light. Look, there is so much in our creativity, in our abilities, that we don't even understand. In this version of scripture, we see how it reads, "the wealth of God's glorious inheritances that He finds IN US" (emphasis mine). When I review these words, it tells me that God sees the wealth that He has placed in us already! God wants you and I to know the wealth that is already in us, the wealth that He sees when He sees us. It is the wealth of His Son and His beautiful creation in us that has given you and me the ability to create.

When you speak, it is the sound of His voice with the power to create. This is our inheritance.

Last thing: notice that you and I are His inheritance, God's inheritance.

ABOVE WHAT WE ASK OR IMAGINE

I don't even know how much more we can dig in with this inheritance. There is gold all over this. In all honesty, there is so much more that I know I haven't uncovered; I have just scratched the surface. YET there is certainly another truth for us in this inheritance that belongs to us. "Now to Him who is able to do above and beyond all that we ask or think according to the power that works in us" (Ephesians 3:20). The King James Version says, "Able to do exceeding abundantly above all that we ask or think," and other translations read, "abundantly more" than we can "imagine." The other version I want to highlight is the Amplified, which says, "Do super abundantly more than all that we dare ask or think [infinitely beyond our greatest prayers, hopes, or dreams]." I believe the Amplified does a great job of explaining what Ephesians 3:20 is saying. God can do WAAAAYYYYY more than we can ever dare dream or ask.

When it comes to the inheritance, it really is about understanding, first and foremost, who God is and next understanding who we are IN HIM and what we have available in Him. We need to ask and use our voices because when we ask according to His will, He is sure to provide (1 John 5:14-15) and do it so much better than we thought He would.

I want to share two short stories with you about how God goes above and beyond because you need to start seeing the whole picture and understand God wants to do more for you than what you ask for. The first story is about my eyes. I have been asking Jesus to heal my eyesight; I walk in complete health, and the only thing I have asked for is to have 20/20 vision. In the journey of knowing Him more, after I asked why I haven't gotten healed with my eyesight, He revealed and showed me my issue is not my eyes at all and that my eyes are healthy. What He revealed to me is what really is happening is deeper than my eyes. He showed me discouragement and depression had kept my brain unable to see life in a joyful way. What was happening in my brain was affecting my sight. He even used Scripture for this: "My eyes grow weary looking for what You have promised; I ask, 'When will you comfort me?'" (Psalm 119:82).

Here I was, asking to have my eyesight healed, yet He said, "I want to do more than that! I want to not only heal your sight. I want to fix your brain, your heart, and your perspective of life." That is the kind of God we have. The kind who wants to do more than we ask. I know that as my perspective shifts, my eyes will align with His truth and be able to see perfectly clearly. Some of us really just need to allow Jesus to fix our brains. I believe this is what keeps us from believing Him and walking in His ways! We THINK we know better; we think that we are the best LOGICAL creatures when, really, He is the Creator who has so much more for us than we even understand. His ways are higher, and His thoughts are higher than ours (Isaiah 55:8-9).

This is our God! Unlike King Ahasuerus, who offered Esther up to half the kingdom, our King is willing to give us above what we ask, think, or imagine. He is even willing to give us the whole earth! Look up the following scriptures and write below!

Psalm 2:8

____

____

Matthew 5:5

____

____

As we see, there are promises where God says that He will give us the whole earth. We ask for nations, and He says, "Here is the whole earth; oh, and by the way, here is My whole kingdom in heaven too." Honestly, this is an awesome God we have. What an inheritance we get for being His sons and daughters.

You see, beloved, it is the will of the Lord to give you His inheritance. It is already done; Ephesians 1:11 reads: "We have also received an inheritance IN HIM, predestined according to the purpose of the One who works out everything in agreement with the decision of His will" (emphasis mine). Our inheritance has already been given; all we need is to believe and receive. To end this, read the following scripture and see that maybe what we need to start doing is *rejoicing in joy* and *boasting of our heritage:* "So that I may enjoy the prosperity of Your chosen ones, rejoice in the joy of Your nation, and boast about Your heritage."

PRAYER

Lord, I thank you so much for the inheritance you have given me. I ask that I may know You more, my true inheritance. May you remove logic from me, that I may believe and see your manifest riches in glory on this earth. Amen.

CHAPTER 7

WISDOM IN HIM

All the treasures of wisdom and knowledge are hidden in Him. —Colossians 2:3

When it comes to wisdom, there is unending insight to cover. In this section, we will include a few items that I felt all work together: wisdom, knowledge, and understanding. First, let me remind you of this one thing: Do not rely on your own understanding. Wisdom in Christ—this wisdom is not of this world; it comes straight from heaven, and it will astonish many on this earth, even the sages of time. See what 1 Corinthians 1:19–25 tells us, then write below who Christ is. And in your own words, explain what God thinks about the wise of this earth.

As we jump into wisdom, we must recognize that our own understanding does not compare to what God wants to share. Some things will not make sense to our human brains, and, therefore, we must have eyes to see and ears to hear. May your eyes open and ears open in Jesus' name.

NO LONGER IN THE FUTILITY OF THE MIND

Ready? Because the LORD has so much to share, but only to those who are seeking and ready to face the truth. The truth is many of us have walked or are still walking in the futility of our minds. With all sincerity, what happens is that our own mind keeps us from believing and seeing the truth. Our mind is also what prevents the move of the Spirit in our own lives. I'm going to give you a word that is probably your worst enemy when it comes to receiving the mind of Christ and the hidden wisdom He keeps for His children. That word? ... *Logic!*

I was reading part of a book written by Ana Mendez-Ferrell, *The Dark Secret of GAOTU: Shattering the Deception of Free Masonry.* In this book, she brings up alchemy, which is sorcery. She exposes that alchemy is introduced by philosophers as "given without falsehood." In other words, that "all is true" of what alchemy says. This is also related to the sciences of the world, which will say only "experiential truth is true and nothing else." She further explains that this is another hindrance to the move of Holy Ghost, which also keeps our minds closed from what Jesus wants to do and even show us.[3] This is all subconscious, programmed in our minds. I know for myself I was such a logical person.

Let me clarify a bit more. Logic is very connected with performance and the "knowing" that if we do something—if we exert a force or energy—there will be a certain reaction. This is Newton's third law, which God can trump, by the way. I'm gonna use the job mentality as an example. Just to make it clear, I am not against jobs because the Lord does call us to work primarily for His glory, not ours. Where I saw logic working in me was with finances, which are connected to jobs. I was in banking for over a decade and went to work at a college where I worked with money as well. Well, in my logical mind, I know that if I put in a certain number of hours at work, I am assured of receiving a certain amount of money to live from. This is logical, am I right?

Well, God wants to break all your logic. He wants to show Himself as the God who is bigger than your own mind. He wants to reveal that He is the God who is wonderful, miraculous, and mighty, the Creator of all. If you are one to be logical, God wants to show you His lordship in your life and break what keeps your mind from seeing His goodness and abundance in your life. When things don't make sense, God is in control. This is what it comes down to—logic tries to tell us that we are in control. This is why there are many Christians who still go on with their lives in frustration, fogginess, and weariness of their future. They are trying to figure everything out, trying to make sense of things. Trust me, I know—I was one of them!

[3] Ana Mendez-Ferrell, The Dark Secret of G.A.O.T.U.: Shattering the Deception of Free Masonry (Pennsylvania, US: Destiny Image, 2011).

Getting back to the truth, what does it even mean to be in the futility of the mind? Let's look at Ephesians 4:17-19.

> Therefore, I say this and testify: You should no longer walk as the Gentiles walk, in the futility of their thoughts. They are darkened in their understanding, excluded from the life of God, because of the ignorance that is in them and because of the hardness of their hearts. They became callous and gave themselves over to promiscuity for the practice of every kind of impurity with a desire for more and more.

I want to share a few ways other versions of scripture describe verse 17: "in the futility of their thinking" (NIV), "for they are hopelessly confused" (NLT), "in the futility of their minds" (ESV), "in the vanity of their mind" (KJV), "in the foolishness and emptiness of their souls" (AMP), "in their empty delusions" (TPT), and last "in their empty rumination" (ARTB).

Let's be real: The futility of the mind is a mind that is full of hopelessness, confusion, emptiness, and foolishness. Empty thoughts that lead nowhere but darkness are the result of a life and mind without the light, Christ Jesus. This futile mind leads to hard hearts and stubbornness, even death. I laugh because I would always say, "I am smart enough to know I don't know it all." Praise God, I was foolish enough to believe Him and what He did on the cross. If that's you too, we no longer are to walk in our previous ways.

Write Ephesians 4:20-21 below:

A wise friend once told me something that I want to share with you. He said, "Maritza, earthly knowledge is great to have; it is important, BUT heavenly wisdom is better." We live in a society that upholds knowledge in such a high regard; to be brutally honest, it's held as an idol. People spend thousands upon thousands of dollars going to college, getting an education, and pursuing knowledge. Just so you know, I did that. I went to college; it's not a bad thing. But there is something better than intellectual knowledge, something that goes further than earthly knowledge as we know it. That something will provide peace in one's decisions and life; that thing is wisdom, God's wisdom.

> No one should deceive himself. If anyone among you thinks he is wise in this age, he must become foolish so that he can become wise.
> —1 Corinthians 3:18

THE BEGINNING OF WISDOM

So many people want wisdom and knowledge but fail to understand how to get it. They fail to understand that it is freely given; it is also up to us to seek it. Look up the two following verses and write both next to them.

Proverbs 1:7

Proverbs 9:10

I have to admit both those scriptures are loaded. When I first read them, I was a bit mystified by them. How is it that the fear of the Lord is the beginning of wisdom? I am not sure about you, but I knew this was deeper than just fear as we know it. When I hear the word fear, it gives the impression of being afraid. The way I have come to know God, I believe He doesn't want us to be afraid of Him but to be able to approach Him—to approach Him with boldness, with praise and thanksgiving. There is one word that resonates with what fear of the Lord is—reverence. The words awe and wonder also are magnified. "Regard or treat with deep respect" is the meaning of reverence, to have reverence for the Lord, to revere Him. In essence, it is to worship Him!

The image I get here is the image of the four living creatures and elders in the book of Revelation, where the elders are casting their crowns before the Lord, falling down before Him.

> Whenever the living creatures give glory, honor, and thanks to the One seated on the throne, the One who lives forever and ever, the 24 elders fall down before the One seated on the throne, worship the One who lives forever and ever, cast their crowns before the throne, and say: Our Lord and God, You are worthy to receive glory and honor and power, because You have created all things, and because of Your will they exist and were created. —Revelation 4:9-11

The creatures and the elders have received the revelation of the fear of the Lord, of His greatness, His power, His beauty, His sovereignty, and majesty. Though they are in the throne room, the fear of the Lord indwells all over them. This is the same fear that came upon Daniel, which made him lose strength, and to Isaiah, that made him say "woe to me" because he saw the Lord.

Worship is essential; it is the breath to the fire. Worship brings reverence before the throne, which brings the revelation and wisdom of the King. Revelation of His Holiness is what prompts us to worship Him more and more! The scripture in Revelation alone gives us instruction on how to worship our God. The first is giving Him honor, glory, and thanks. This postures us to give true worship and receive wisdom and knowledge and revelation. I said a word that is important and caught my attention as I wrote. That word is posture; to posture our hearts is going to be the only way for us to receive the fear of the Lord, wisdom, and revelation.

I want to remind you of Proverbs 1:7, which tells us, "The fear of the Lord is the beginning of knowledge; fools despise wisdom and discipline." We are reminded that fools despise wisdom and discipline. It is fools who will fall into pride and fools who dislike discipline. In the book of Proverbs, there are many scriptures about humility. Humility and humbling ourselves is crucial, for it is what will allow us to posture our hearts in such a way that will invite the fear of the Lord, the honoring of Him; anything else is pride, which is the only thing that will surely repel His presence. Look up Proverbs 11:2 and write it below:

I want to touch on humility because it is an important move on our behalf for wisdom, understanding, and knowledge. In fact, I would say it is required to receive the wisdom that comes from above. There is no other way. Proverbs 22:4 tells us that the result of humility is the fear of the Lord, and as we just covered, fear of the Lord is the beginning of wisdom. Humility is not being humiliated. Let us make that clear! *Humility is having a teachable spirit and being able to submit to authority,* and the book of Ephesians does a great job explaining submission for those who want to read further. I will add that humility is also the ability to receive correction without being offended, angry, or even full-on rebelling. It is asking forgiveness when needed. It is admitting we don't know it all and admitting that God is God and He does know best. When we finally confess we need wisdom, then we can ask! James 1:5 says, "Now if any of you lacks wisdom, he should ask God, who gives to all generously and without criticizing, and it will be given to him." Look, Scripture tells us that God gives wisdom generously. But for us to receive this wisdom, there is something we must do, which we will find if we read further; it tells us to "ask in faith without doubting" (James 1:6). God honors our request when we ask in faith and when we lay aside pride and criticism, only when we come humbly knowing that He will do it.

The key to wisdom is humility.

BEAUTY AND TREASURE

I am going to pose this question, which you really don't have to answer—but humor me. Ever wonder why a good-looking man or woman can instantly become ugly when evil comes out of their mouths? I must admit I had to chuckle when this thought came to mind. How dare I, as a Christian, as a follower of Jesus, as a child of God, say that someone is ugly? I dare because there is truth to that question. I'm going to share a scripture that speaks about what wisdom does: "She will place a garland of grace on your head; she will give you a crown of beauty" (Proverbs 4:9). When I read that, the posed question suddenly made so much sense. When we speak, we reveal what is inside our hearts; we show what we are really made of, ugliness or beauty. Now that we know where beauty truly comes from and we have asked for wisdom, it is time for us to become beautiful. We beautify ourselves through wisdom. We seek wisdom and do what the fear of the Lord prompts us to do. The whole book of Proverbs gives us the instruction of what it means to be wise; I would highly recommend that book. The book of Proverbs is, hands down, a passage of Scripture that has an abundance of golden nuggets on wisdom. King Solomon, the primary writer of Proverbs, knew to ask for wisdom above everything else. The Psalms also have great insight on wisdom; one is Psalm 37. Go and read this, and as you read this chapter, write down the instructions it gives us, for the title of this Psalm in my HCSB Bible is "Instruction in Wisdom."

This psalm is so beautiful, with direct instruction from God to us. It touches on giving up anger and rage, but one command that I believe is so important and many overlook is in the very first verse. This is "do not envy." Though we read in that verse that we are to not envy those who do wrong, I would take it further and say, "Do not envy—period." It shouldn't matter who it is; we should not envy anyone. Jealousy is straight evil, inviting strife and lies in your life, not wisdom. This is what James 3:16 has to say about the matter: "For where envy and selfish ambition exists, there is disorder and every kind of evil." Psalm 37 directs us in verse 27 to turn away from evil.

Envy = Evil

If you experience envy, I want to say first, there is no shame; second, ask yourself why you feel this way. I will admit when I felt envy and jealousy, the Lord revealed the reasons, and most of this came from a place of lack of love. Remember, the spirit of wisdom is that of the God who is love. I would suggest the same, to ask if there is rage and anger, where this is coming from because that is not coming from the God of love.

The last direction I want to cover is watching our mouths. I do hope you read the book of Proverbs, as I already mentioned. In it, you will repeatedly read what the wise person's mouth expresses and what the mouth of a foolish person spews and causes. I already covered in the chapter on peace about how God would ask me not to speak, to keep my mouth shut. Look, I was being straight-up foolish. The mouth of the wise is to speak no idle word. We are to only utter words from heaven that bring healing, teaching, guidance, and life to those around us.

Let us go to Isaiah 6:1–7; read these verses and pay attention to Isaiah's response. What does he say about his mouth, and what happens next?

Isaiah got to see the holiness of the Lord; he got to be in the throne room and see the beauty of the Lord. He recognized that his mouth was unclean; his response caused the angel to act. We then observe the seraphim angel take away the wickedness from Isaiah's lips with the coal. This is such a holy moment—no condemnation, only purity and love from the throne room. Many of us need to allow God or angels to touch our lips with the glowing coal from the altar, allow Him to tell us to be silent for a while, or even just choose to stop speaking nonsense. If we want wisdom, though it is freely given, we must also acknowledge that there is action on our end.

Those are the first steps to gaining wisdom, understanding, and revelation. Consider the verse that starts us in this chapter on wisdom: "All the treasures of wisdom and knowledge are hidden in Him" (Colossians 2:3). I'm telling you, Jesus is the answer to it all. We seek Him, and when we find Him, He reveals more of who He is, and indeed He is wisdom. Notice the verse in Colossians gives us the word treasures. We are to seek, ask, and knock. Though God gives us wisdom, we are to still seek HIM, read His Word, commune with Him, and be in His presence. It is in His presence where treasures are made known, where the hidden things are revealed.

Find the following verses and write what these scriptures say wisdom is better than.

Proverbs 3:14-15 ______________________________

Proverbs 8:11 ______________________________

Proverbs 16:16 ______________________________

Let's be honest—if someone told you that they know where a treasure is hidden with gold, silver, and jewels, you would be like, "Let's go get it!" Can I inform you that I am here right now telling you: I know of a treasure that holds an essence that is better than rubies, better than silver, and better than gold! I also know where it is hidden! It is hidden in Him, in Christ Jesus. We are to search for it in the Word and in Him.

PRAISE GOD WHO HOLDS ALL WISDOM

> May the name of God be praised forever and ever, for wisdom and power belong to Him. —Daniel 2:20

In Him, we find everything we need. This is the beauty of being in Him. When we have questions, we go to Him. Jesus tells us in Matthew 13:11 that the secrets of heaven have been made known to us but not to everyone. He says, "It has not been given to them." Who is *them?* "Them" are those who still walk in the futility of their minds—those who are still foolish, walking and talking wickedness, those who are not children of God but of the devil. To further solidify this, Deuteronomy 29:29 states: "The hidden things belong to the Lord our God, but the revealed things belong to us and our children forever so that we may follow all the words of this law." It is only those who follow the statutes of the Lord who get the revelation of the hidden things.

There is one man in the Bible who knew the importance of seeking He who is wisdom. This is a man whom we can all learn from; he understood the importance of staying in God's presence until he received revelation. He also would not compromise, staying faithful to the Lord in everything, which, in turn, gave him favor before kings and not just any king—pagan kings. This man is Daniel. There is so much we can learn from Daniel about our God, who holds all wisdom; we can learn how to live a life that is consecrated, sanctified, and holy, set apart for His will. Read Daniel 2:19-30.

Now that you read that notice what Daniel's response is in verses 27 and 28. What does he tell us?

____

Daniel knew the mightiness of the Lord. He didn't just know that God is mighty; Daniel was confident in who the Lord is! He knew he could go to the Lord, the God who reveals mysteries. Daniel knew how to live in Him, how to dwell in Him through prayer, fasting, seeking, and not backing down to a society that lured him with the best the world had to offer in his day. He knew exactly who to go to in time of need, in time of joy, in time of sorrow, in every single day of his life, which is why God trusted him with such wisdom and power.

This is the reason this wisdom is only given to those who seek, to those who make themselves ready for it. If we read the beginning of the book of Daniel, we find that he consecrated himself and chose not to defile himself. He purified himself. Truly, I believe this is why the Lord spoke to Daniel. He saw a man who had faith in the God of heaven.

Brother and sister, praise God! Praise the Lord, who gives us wisdom. Praise God that He tells us to ask and that He is always there for us, just waiting for us to turn to Him, waiting for us to *believe* Him—to believe that He is the God that He says He is. He is everything! In this story, He is the God who reveals mysteries, the God who changes times and seasons, the God who holds the whole earth and defies the laws of man. He is the God who speaks, the God who is ever-present, showing us what is to come, speaking to us always. We even see our God speak to a Babylonian king through dreams! He speaks to everyone because He wants to be known; He wants you and me to come to Him and seek the mysteries of heaven that are given to us, the secrets that are revealed to us when we seek them for what they are: treasure.

> May the name of God be praised forever and ever, for wisdom and power belong to Him. He changes the times and seasons; He removes kings and establishes kings. He gives wisdom to the wise and knowledge to those who have understanding. He reveals the deep and hidden things; He knows what is in the darkness, and light dwells with Him. I offer thanks and praise to You, God of my fathers, because You have given me wisdom and power. And now You have let me know what we asked of You, for You have let us know the king's mystery. —Daniel 2:20–23

In later chapters, we see Daniel seeking the Lord many more times. One case is when there is writing on the wall, and God gives him the interpretation. Another time, an angel was sent to him with an answer to prayer. I want you to see how Daniel was described because of God's wisdom revealed to him, for he sought the Lord: "In the days of your predecessor he was found to have insight, intelligence, and wisdom like the wisdom of the gods" (Daniel 5:11).

How awesome is this? Don't you want to be known like that? I know I do—not because of my own intelligence but because I know the God who is wisdom. This same wisdom is available to you if you ask in faith and believe in Him.

There is so much wealth in this book I can go on and on. The last statement I want to make is this: Daniel never took the glory; he always made sure everyone he spoke to with interpretations knew that it was GOD who gave the understanding.

WISDOM, UNDERSTANDING, REVELATION

There is a statement that Daniel used to describe the Lord, the Revealer of Mysteries. Our God is so vast our own minds cannot comprehend. As I heard someone mention once, "He is too big for my puny brain." This is why our earthly wisdom does not suffice in this walk with Christ; it is our own minds that get in the way. We must learn to be in Him, allowing the Spirit to overtake us, to possess us, so that we may indeed receive the mind of Christ, which has already been given to us who believe.

There is a shift that happens as we mature in wisdom, as we lay down our pride. As we come before God, knowing we are weak and knowing we need Him, it allows us to step into greater revelation and greater glory of God, where we begin to see, hear and understand His wisdom. Where we do just like the elders and angels do—join in and begin to truly sing holy, holy, holy. Where we get to experience the throne room and receive the revelation of the mysteries that belong to us as His children because we begin to live as He does. We begin to live a life full of wonder, reverence, and adoration for the King. We become childlike, seeking the treasure, full of excitement.

The King only reveals these mysteries to those whom He will trust and those whom He knows will honor Him and His will. Psalm 25:14 says, "The secret counsel of the Lord is for those who fear Him, and He reveals His covenant to them." The wisdom, revelation, and mysteries are not for us to take and plaster all over the world; there are some mysteries reserved for those He loves only. The bridegroom will not take everyone into the bridal chamber. The King will only give certain information to His adviser; the Father will only give certain gifts to His children. We break through the threshold and the veil when we realize that knowledge only goes so far. Though I knew what Scripture would tell me about my position in Christ, it did nothing for me until I surrendered my mind to God to hear His voice and see what He sees. Here is when we begin to do what 1 Corinthians 2:7 states: "We speak God's hidden wisdom in a mystery, a wisdom God predestined before the ages of our glory." Only through surrender can we reach that.

I want to touch one more time on Revelation chapter 4. Read this whole chapter and notice the revelation John experiences because he believed.

Notice what verse 2 says: John was in the Spirit! This is important for us to grasp. We cannot do anything without the Holy Spirit.

Write 1 Corinthians 2:13 here.

It is only by the Spirit that we can come to the knowledge of Him. Only through the Holy Spirit can we access and receive the mind of Christ by faith and be in the heavenly realm.

> "But we have the mind of Christ." —1 Corinthians 2:16

John allowed the Spirit to bring him through that door and see the throne—to be in the throne room and experience the throne. He got the revelation of the creatures around the throne room, he saw the rainbow, he saw the Ancient of Days who carries all wisdom, the One who was and is and is to come! The One with no beginning and no end because He is the beginning and the end. John saw the elders who fell before the Lamb, worshiped, and continually shouted, "He is worthy to receive glory and honor and power" because He has created all things, and because of His will, all things exist and were created!

I pray that one day, you too, will get this revelation of the throne. I know that many people write about it. I have to admit that one time, I heard someone I honor and respect mention that he likes it when people actually live out the life of God and not just write about it. I pondered on his statement since I was in the middle of writing this book. I bring this up to say, yes, I have experienced the throne.

The first time I ever did was impactful. When I was at a prayer meeting in which I knew there was a witch present, I recall being on my knees and singing spiritual songs with my arms raised, praising the Lord. At first, I was a bit concerned, but the following was the best. I could see I was on the sea of glass, and then God showed me I was a portal, a gate to bring heaven to the prayer room. He then said to me, "Maritza, you are in the throne room with me. She has no access here; she can't touch you. Just remain here." Trust me, I wouldn't be writing any of these words in these pages if it wasn't that God had spoken them. I pray that God gives you this kind of understanding and more, the revelation of who He truly is and that you may come to love Him and honor Him as He loves you.

We praise the Lord, and we worship Him with reverence before His throne, allowing Him to change us that we may become more like Him and less like us. ALL of ourselves, for ALL of Him that we may walk this earth with His wisdom, showing the true power He is.

In ending this chapter, I want you to see the promises that are available, ones that Paul wrote about in a prayer just for you. Look up Ephesians 3:15-19 and write it out for yourself, then read it and post it somewhere you see it every day if need be.

PRAYER

Lord, Thank you that you give us all wisdom and understanding in you. I come before you with humility, exposing any pride in me. I want to know you, I want to see you, and I want the revelation of who you are. Make known to me the mystery of your will according to your good pleasure that you have planned in you. In Jesus' name. Amen.

CHAPTER 8

CONFIDENCE IN HIM

We have boldness through him, and free access as kings before the Father because of our complete confidence in Christ's faithfulness. —Ephesians 3:12 TPT

This section we are starting has been the hardest to write for me. Finding the words to help you understand was challenging. To be quite honest, it is because I myself was learning how to walk confidently in the Lord, firm and *truly unshaken!* I believe many people walk this life a bit dazed, confused, or even trembling at the knees; that was me. About three years ago, I was introduced to someone who, when I saw this person, I recall thinking, *Wow, this guy is FEARLESS!* I wanted that. I wanted to walk in such a manner. He carried himself with authority, and he knew who he was and was not shaken by what others thought—or even by any threats from the enemy. After being mentored by him for the last three years, I can indeed stand on that initial statement and praise Jesus that this man is raising up fearless leaders.

That is the first thing about confidence—there is no fear in confidence!

Scripture tells us that perfect love casts out fear (1 John 4:18), and I will be covering how love is the firm foundation to walk confidently and the only way we can truly be fearless.

UNSHAKEN

When it comes to confidence, I would use this word to describe it: UNSHAKEN. This means to walk in such boldness that nothing shakes you, nothing will make you back down, nothing will make you coward, and nothing will make you shrink back. Boldness is present, and you stand tall; as you may notice, this is also describing *fearless*. To be fearless is to be unshaken.

I am going to go straight into it. There are a few things God revealed about having confidence in Him. The main fruit that will bring forth confidence is His love. There truly is nothing like His love. I want us to look at the following scripture: "For the king relies on the Lord; through the faithful love of the Most High he is not shaken" (Psalm 21:7). This scripture is rich in showing how to remain unshaken. We see King David in this verse disclose how, through the *faithful love* of the Most High, he is *not shaken*. David even shares how he relies on the Lord; he reveals that it is His love that keeps him unshaken. The love of the Lord is the "secret" to be unshaken. His love is so powerful; His Word says that perfect love casts out all fear! It is fear that weakens our knees, causing them to tremble and causing us to be shaken; we quiver, we doubt, and we shrink back. When we fear, we lack confidence in whatever it is we are out to accomplish.

Let me share this with you. I worked at a community college for a while. During my time there, I worked in a department that helped those with "barriers" or who were in transitions of life. By barriers, academia would describe them as those with housing insecurity, English as a second language, people with a record, or those with food insecurity, amongst other things. Before I proceed, I must also mention that I was in charge of a pilot program in which I tracked students for the length of their training from beginning to end. I was one to help them, encourage them, and make sure they were in class. I was a go-to person, an adviser, and an advocate for them. What I came to quickly observe is that because of their life situations, they lacked confidence in themselves. They lacked confidence because they never had someone in their lives say something as simple as, "You can do this," or "I believe in you," let alone someone to show they cared about them.

In my first book, *Loved by Love: How Love Restores a Heart*, I mention how an aspect of love is showing the one you love that you care about them. To love is to care about another person. In my situation, I thought no one cared about me, which led me to think I was unloved, and this brought so much fear into my life. I was absolutely bound by fear, which caused me to feel beyond shaken in all areas of my life. I would say I was paralyzed by fear, unable to even take a step forward. This is exactly what I saw in those students I helped. There was a lack of love in their lives. They felt unworthy or not enough; confidence was missing. All I had to do was be a present person to tell them that I believed in them and that I was there for them. Confidence came when they realized someone was there for them, they were valued, and they mattered.

In the same way for me, confidence came when I learned that God, the God of love, loves me. We find David saying the same thing in the verse we just reviewed: "For the king relies on the Lord; through the faithful love of the Most High he is not shaken."

The key to being confident is HIS faithful love!

Look up Psalm 27:3, then write it out and speak it over yourself.

EVERLASTING BOND

Since I was having such a challenge to write this section of confidence, God told me to look at the last chapter of my first book, which I mentioned earlier. I did as instructed, and lo and behold, the title of that last chapter: "Confidence in Love." What a major confirmation of the Lord telling us that His love is crucial for our confidence! In that book, I wrote about having a sense of security when we know we belong to God. When we know His love is for us, we walk stately and secure. As I was reading that chapter, I realized that God wanted to go deeper! He wants you and I to go from knowing we are loved to believing we are loved to *BEING* loved. Most importantly, we are to understand who we are loved by and what it really means.

I want to share a statement I wrote in a journal.

> "Your love; your covenant love of marriage over me. Your covenant is true; it is unbroken, forever strong, forever faithful. You don't break your covenant; you hold it to the end. Thank you for your covenant; praise you for your faithfulness." (Maritza 5/12/21)

I want to acknowledge that some of you reading this have gone through divorce or are experiencing brokenness in your marriage. You may even look at what I wrote and mock it, thinking that this marriage thing or covenant of marriage is nonsense. Well, before you keep mocking or wanting to skip over this, because trust me, I have skipped over things like this before, I am asking you to stay with me here. I am declaring to you that there is a bond of love that comes from the Lord that can never be broken, one that remains forever and ever and ever! God calls it a covenant.

His covenant of love—not a man made agreement but a covenant that is from the heavens and is sealed by HIS BLOOD.

In earlier chapters, I have spoken about communion elements. Well, now that you are here in this place of confidence, let me tell you that communion with the Lord is entering into covenant with Him! A covenant always involves the flesh and the blood. This is the consummation of a marriage, even in the physical realm of man and woman; why would God be any different? He is the One who created marriage. We are to consume Him!

Recently, in my studies about covenant, I learned that kingship was also established with a covenant! Find 2 Samuel 5:1-3; read it, and write down what the tribes of Israel tell David.

This is full of power; I pray you feel the depth of this as I do. In marriage, the bride comes to the bridegroom, and they become one flesh. What has Jesus done on the cross but give HIS flesh and blood for us! He even said the following: "The one who eats My flesh and drinks My blood lives in Me, and I in him" (John 6:56). Clearly, we see that we become one in Christ by consuming the flesh and blood, Him in us and us in Him, one flesh. We come into a marriage covenant with the Lord Himself, and we come into the kingship of Jesus.

Look up 2 Samuel 23:5 and write out what David once again says to the Lord.

God has *established* His covenant.

MORE ON THE COVENANT

This section of confidence is so important because it is what we can stand on when it comes to His love, which is why I want to cover a few other important aspects of God's covenant. Let us look at this next scripture: "He will not leave you, destroy you, or forget the covenant with your fathers that He swore to them by oath, because the Lord your God is a compassionate God." (Deuteronomy 4:31). In this verse we just read, I would like to highlight a few things. One, it says that God will not forget the covenant that He swore by oath. Two, it was a covenant made with "your fathers," which speaks of generational blessing and how an everlasting God will not break His promises.

Look up the following passages of scripture and read them: Genesis 9:12-17 and then Isaiah 59:21.

There is something I want you to grasp in these two sections of Scripture, which tie into the one in Deuteronomy. First, in Genesis 9:15-16, the Lord mentions that whenever the bow, or the rainbow, appears, He will look at it and remember the everlasting covenant He made! So not only did God create the rainbow for us to remember His covenant but also for Him to remember. A fun fact about the rainbow is that the rainbow surrounds the throne in heaven, meaning it is always in His sight! He will never forget! The second thing I want to emphasize is with Isaiah 59:21, Genesis 9:12, and Deuteronomy 4:31, where God speaks of this covenant for all future generations, meaning that His covenant is everlasting; it doesn't stop with Abraham or Noah or even David. The covenant is for us and our children's children and their children's children.

As if that isn't enough, let us just end with one more truth on the covenant before we delve deeper into confidence. Remember that the covenant is the firm foundation for walking in confidence, which is why I am taking time with this. Let us now look at the ark of the covenant. Everything about the Bible is so intentional. God is wonderful with details, which is why He was very specific with the building of the ark of the covenant. Read Exodus 25:10-22, for I will not cover all the details. What I will focus on are the elements used to create the ark: acacia wood and pure gold. What I learned is acacia wood is very strong, rot-resistant, and lasts generations. The very substance of the ark of the covenant was created to last generations. Even in this, God shows us that He is serious about His covenant; it is one to last past our own existence on this earth. The fact that it is strong and rot-resistant represents how His very covenant is strong and will not allow anything to weaken it or bring death to it. As for the gold, it, too, is "durable to the point of virtual indestructibility."[4]

It is a wonder to attain these details because it shows that God, indeed, is very intentional about His covenant with us. He truly means what He means. There is absolutely nothing in this world that will break His covenant, which He created. It truly is a firm foundation for us to walk on, and we can trust Him because of His indestructible covenant with us.

This brings Romans 8:38-39 to mind: "For I am persuaded that not even death or life, angels or rulers, things present or things to come, hostile powers, height or depth, or any other created thing will have the power to separate us from the love of God that is in Christ Jesus our Lord!"

[4] "Gold," Britannica, https://www.britannica.com/science/gold-chemical-element.

HIS CHARACTER BRINGS TRUST

There is something we can say about knowing someone. Is there anyone in this world that you know without a shadow of a doubt that would come help if you called them? I'm guessing there is someone you can think of who would do just that—drop everything and come help. That is the same way our relationship with the Lord works. When we know Him, and I mean KNOW Him—not just know *of* Him, but know Him—everything changes, and we are able to trust Him.

Trust is really a way to say, "Lord, my confidence is in you; even when I do not understand, I will take that step forward." Let's look at what Jeremiah 17:7 says, "The man who trusts in the Lord, whose confidence indeed is the Lord, is blessed." It is applying even Proverbs 3:5 in your life to trust in the Lord with ALL your heart and not lean on your own understanding. The question is how? How can we do this? The Word alone should be enough for us believers, but I want to help you get this rooted: *We come to trust HIS character and believe with all our hearts that He is who He says He is.*

Search out Psalm 25:1-11 and read it.

In these words of Scripture, we find David once again praying to the Lord. Notice his prayer. Though he was crying out, in verses one and two, we find him start by saying the following words: "Lord, I turn to You. My God, I trust in You." He begins his petition by telling the Lord that he trusts Him no matter his circumstances. Then, in verses six through eleven, we find David reminding the Lord of HIS character. We find David telling the Lord to remember HIS compassion and His faithful love and then proceeding to tell the Lord who He is, "The Lord is good and upright." At the end of this excerpt, David even says, "Because of your name, Yahweh." We can all learn from David; we can see David KNEW the Lord. David was able to remind the Lord of His majesty, of His unfailing, faithful love, and of His goodness. David never once said, as I once did, "Because of my obedience to you, God, because I am good." This is because it is not about our character; it is about God and His glory! We even read that David, unlike me at the time, recognized His own shortcomings; he told God *to not remember* his sins. David knew his own wickedness yet also knew the Lord's love. He didn't just believe in the love of God; he knew His love and trusted it could overcome.

I would like to suggest that David already had a track record of the Lord's faithfulness, and David would remember what the Lord has done for him. Even now, I would highly recommend that as you are reading this, remember all the good things God has done for you!

Create your own prayer below, reminding God of His character for your cry.

THE SONSHIP ACCEPTANCE

As mentioned previously, what has been covered thus far of our confidence in Him is really the firm foundation of His faithful love. Knowing Him and His character is equally as important. We must enter that covenant of love to know Him, and with that comes the confidence in this next area of our life with God that drives our roots in Him even deeper—our acceptance in Christ as sons and daughters.

Before I move forward, I want you to observe the following promises and, in your own words, write what they say to you. Read John 14:17–18.

In the section on inheritance, we already touched on the subject of orphans, and here again, we must briefly touch on it. Jesus is speaking, telling us first that we have the Spirit of truth, whom we know, and then He will not leave us as orphans but instead is coming to us! Again, in Romans 8:15–17, we see that we received the Spirit of adoption by whom we cry out, "Abba, Father!" As we continue further in Romans, it reads, "The Spirit Himself testifies together with our spirit we are God's children, and if children also heirs—heirs of God and coheirs with Christ." I want you to see Romans 8:19, "For the creation eagerly waits with anticipation for God's sons to be revealed."

Throughout this whole journey, my goal has been to help you understand what you carry with Christ, in Him. There is something powerful with this aspect of sonship. I want to share the following words that were uttered by Prophet Charlie Shamp in a teaching: "The backbone of dominion is sonship."[5] When I hear of backbone, I hear of one who will stand tall and not back down when opposition comes. We also have the word *dominion* in that statement. Look at what Genesis 1:28 says: "God blessed them, and God said to them, 'Be fruitful, multiply, fill the earth, and *subdue* it. Rule the fish of the sea, the birds of the sky, and every creature that crawls on the earth." God has blessed us to take dominion of the earth; He tells us to subdue it. It truly makes sense why, in Romans 8:19, creation eagerly waits for the sons to be revealed! For it is the sons of God, the ones who walk in sonship, who understand their call to take dominion of the earth and bring it back to its original state with heaven. For if we read in Romans 8:21, it says, "That the creation itself will also be set free from the bondage of corruption into the glorious freedom of God's children." As sons and daughters, God has given us *full authority* and *dominion* over all the earth.

When we come into the acceptance of our sonship in Christ and walk as sons and daughters, not as orphans, that is when we can walk in confidence because we have

[5] From an online video teaching by Prophet Charlie Shamp.

been given the power from our heavenly Father, who watches over His children. This is a level of confidence we have in Him, full of dominion.

Think about it: dominion, where we dominate every element on the earth in the spirit and all around, means that everything is under our feet, just as it is under the feet of Jesus. Even Jesus uttered the words, "Look, I have given you the authority to trample on snakes and scorpions and over all the power of the enemy; nothing will ever harm you" (Luke 10:19). We trample on the snakes, scorpions, and demons, crushing anything that tries to keep us in fear. There will be no more fear because, in acceptance of sonship, it is our right to walk in dominion. THAT is powerful.

VICTORIOUS AUTHORITY

There is one last thing I want to share about the ability to walk in confidence in Him. This is more of the cherry on top of everything we have already covered; it is our inheritance, and we shouldn't forget about it. There are three things I want to mention that we have access to for protection and guidance as we walk boldly toward the destiny God has for us.

The first one is we have the angelic army with us, which we are to co-labor with; they are here to help us. Find Hebrews 1:14 and write it out.

____

____

Who are those who inherit salvation? You and me. We inherited salvation, and with it, we get angels to help and serve us to fulfill God's calling in our lives and bring heaven to earth, not for our fleshly desires. When I heard this about the angels and the host of heaven being on our side, all I could think of was this one line from the movie *Tombstone*, but instead replacing the word "hell" with heaven! "Tell them I'm coming, and heaven is coming with me, you hear?!" That's how we should be, so bold and confident that when the enemy tries to attack, we say, "Heaven is coming with me!" and we don't back down; we stand our ground and move forward.

The next thing we have with us we have already covered, but I will mention it because I am not sure we have talked about its power to protect, and that is the blood of Jesus. I can't even begin with this; it is so holy and precious. For a great teaching on the blood, Billye Brim has some resources.[6] I know more are out there, but I recall a story she shared about drawing a blood line on her property. By drawing a blood

[6] From The Blood and the Glory (Harrison House, 1998) and The Authority of the Believer and How to Use It (Billye Brim Ministries, Audio, 2016).

line, I don't mean going out there and taking a marker and drawing your property, no. What I mean is in prayer and in the Spirit, all she said was, "I claim the blood of Jesus over my property all around the border." (I will add that taking the physical communion elements with your land is an act of faith at work too.) What transpired is that the devil had told her he was going to kill her family, and immediately she prayed the blood line by faith. In the morning, what did she find at the borderline of her property? Foxes that were infected with rabies—dead. She tells the story better, of course, but from the day I heard that story back in 2016, I have held on to that truth about the blood!

I'll share a brief story on this of my own. In short, when I was living alone, there was a man who was stalking me. I mean, for real, he was; this guy was not supposed to be on premises, and police were involved. In the Spirit, the first time I ever saw that man, I literally heard "lust and witchcraft." I share this to show you that instantly, I knew this was a spiritual battle. I can honestly say I felt fear because I could feel the wickedness in this man; it was strong. BUT GOD! God used this to teach me how to stand strong and not lose peace in my own home. There was harassment, and this person found out exactly where I lived. One evening, I was thinking about this man and what I should do. Holy Spirit in me started speaking to me and instructed me to declare these words: "I claim the blood of Jesus over my 900 square foot apartment, and I thank you, Lord, for the angels in my home and outside on post." No joke—nine minutes later (yes, nine minutes, I remember; you never forget things like this), I heard a knock at my door, and who was it? Yes, that man full of demons. Was my flesh fearful? At that moment, what transpired was my spirit man rose up, and I knew that I knew I was beyond protected! I knew.

Look, after that, I was telling the Lord that if I had a man in the house, this would never happen. Can I tell you what God said? This is what the Lord of lords said: "Really, Maritza? What can a human man do? Do you not know that I protect better than a man can? Do you not know that? Look, I have given you the blood of Jesus, the angels, and the Holy Spirit."

The enemy had come to shake me, to scare me from stepping into my destiny; I had already gone out to Africa, where I got to be part of deliverance and healing ministries, so I have seen this kind of stuff. The enemy was scared, so he came to my home to try to scare me. It worked for three days; I was shaken, yet the Lord was with me all along, speaking to me and showing me how to not back down and showing me my power and authority in Him.

There are two more things I'd like to share with you in regard to confidence. One is Holy Spirit, who the Lord mentioned to me the day that man knocked at my door. Oh man, I don't know what I would do without Holy Spirit. I couldn't even go to the mailbox without Him. Holy Spirit is so amazing. He is the counselor and the One who speaks truth, giving insight into the physical realm and the spirit realm. He also tells us of the things to come when we are in relationship with Him. Write out the following scriptures below and see how Holy Spirit is the One who fills you with power and boldness.

Acts 1:8

Acts 4:31

Last but not least, the Word. The Word is prominent because it is part of us partaking in the covenant. When we partake of the flesh, it means partaking of the Word. John 1:14 says, "The Word became flesh and took up residence among us. WE observed His glory, the glory as the One and Only Son from the Father, full of grace and truth" (emphasis mine). We can stand on His Word that never returns void; He watches over it! "The Lord said to me, 'You have seen correctly, for I watch over My word to accomplish it'" (Jeremiah 1:12). This is our weapon, our sword to cut the enemy and fight back.

GO IN CONFIDENCE

There is such confidence in knowing we are marked by God, set apart, loved, and called His. The God of all calls us His and will do anything for His beloved, for His bride. With that, we may keep walking forward in this world with full acceptance, with complete love, with the hosts of angels and Holy Ghost knowing we are equipped and truly nothing can touch us when we believe wholeheartedly. Here it is again: "Look, I have given you the authority to trample on snakes and scorpions and over all the power of the enemy; nothing will ever harm you. However, don't rejoice that the spirits submit to you, but rejoice that your names are written in heaven" (Luke 10:19-20).

With all we have covered, we can rest securely in Christ. "Then you would trust [with confidence], because there is hope; you would look around you and rest securely" (Job 11:18, AMP). We can trust the Word when it says, "Nothing will ever harm you." Say this with me: "It is finished; I am bold; I am confident; I am unshaken; I am secure; I am worthy to walk my calling; I am powerful in Him."

Let us finish with this wonderful Psalm we can all stand on.

PSALM 16: CONFIDENCE IN THE LORD

> Protect me, God, for I take refuge in You.
> I said to Yahweh, "You are my Lord; I have nothing good besides You."
> As for the holy people who are in the land, they are the noble ones. All my delight is in them. The sorrows of those who take another god for themselves will multiply; I will not pour out their drink offerings of blood, and I will not speak their names with my lips. Lord, You are my portion and my cup of blessing; You hold my future. The boundary lines have fallen for me in pleasant places; indeed, I have a beautiful inheritance.
>
> I will praise the Lord who counsels me—even at night my conscience instructs me. I keep the Lord in mind always.
> Because He is at my right hand, I will not be shaken.
>
> Therefore, my heart is glad and my spirit rejoices; my body also rests securely. For You will not abandon me to Sheol; You will not allow Your Faithful One to see decay. You reveal the path of life to me; in Your presence is abundant joy; in Your right hand are eternal pleasures.

PRAYER

Thank you, Jesus, for your unfailing and everlasting love. Thank you for loving me and the ability to rest in your faithfulness. Let your love wash over me afresh today. May any shakiness in my knees be strengthened with your love. Amen.

CHAPTER 9

LIFE IN HIM

For you have died, and your life is hidden with the Messiah in God. —Colossians 3:3

"In the Beginning was the Word, and the Word was with God, and the Word was God. He was with God in the beginning. All things were created through Him, and apart from Him not one thing was created that has been created. Life was in Him, and that life was the light of men. That light shines in the darkness, yet the darkness did not overcome it" (John 1:1–5).

We are nearing the end of this journey of walking in Him together. Of course, it is my desire you continue to grow on your own once you are done reading this book. It is amazingly wonderful how God leads. We started the pages of this book with "it is finished," the words Jesus spoke before giving up His last breath so that He may bring us back to the beginning. Now, as we are nearing the end, we go to "in the beginning." Back to the beginning. Back to the Garden, back to being full of life in Christ. Back to being full of the light because any darkness that was with you when you first opened this print has started to leave—because the light shines, and the darkness cannot and did not overcome it!

I am going to share two personal journal entries I bumped into as I was just going through some of my old journals during February of 2023.

> "Do I just have a dark point of view? Maybe inside my heart there is still darkness? I need your kindness, love, and warmth. Help me see the beauty in my life." (Journal entry 11/28/20)

> "I feel so dead; where has the excitement gone? Where has the expectancy gone? Where has the joy gone? Where are the bubbles? Where are the swirls? Where are the sparkles and the rainbows? Most of all, where is the sun? The light? The warmth?" (Journal entry 3/26/22)

I wonder if you noticed what I noticed. Note the very first question in that first journal entry and then how I end with the last two questions in the second entry. As I wrote these entries, I was pouring my heart out to God, asking genuinely; I wrote as I thought, and as I look back, I realize that, indeed, I still had a dark point of view in many areas of my life. I was blinded by the lens of disappointment, unable to see the light. I needed a change of perspective in the light. I share this because the word we just read in John says, "Life was in Him, and that life was the light of men" (1:4). I was asking for excitement; I was asking for the sparkles and the rainbows. In essence, as I look back, I was dead in life. I was only existing. I didn't have excitement for life, yet my heart was asking for it. I wanted to be alive again! I asked for the light at the time, not realizing that life is in the light.

You guys, we need the light to live. When we think about plants, we know they require light to live. As a plant needs light, so do we, so we may flourish in all areas of our destiny. Step fully into the light where no darkness resides, where you can get a new lens and perspective—the lens of gratitude and love.

FROM DEATH TO LIFE

Jesus explains He is the Way, the Truth, and the Life (John 14:6). There is no other way to the Father, who is God. Life is God; He is eternal life. Jesus explains in Matthew 10:39, "Anyone finding his life will lose it, and anyone losing his life because of Me will find it." I think many people ponder how to get there. As we explore more scriptures, we can see some things will have to pass away for the new to come.

Let's look at that staple scripture I have referred to many times and may do so a few more times before the end of these pages:

> I have been crucified with Christ and I no longer live, but Christ lives in me. The life I now live in the body, I live by faith in the Son of God, who loved me and gave Himself for me. —Galatians 2:19-20

Galatians reads being "crucified with Christ." This informs us there is an instruction—an instruction of us being crucified, of us losing our lives that we may live. We *must* give the Lord the dead parts of our hearts for Him to bring back life into those areas of our hearts. Even as I write this, God has been reviving places of my heart. Due to the disappointment I mentioned, I had not only let dreams die but I made sure they were buried deep, deep down in my heart—and I mean deep! I walked around carrying death in my heart; I was full of anger and bitterness because of this disappointment. I really didn't think God cared for me or even loved me. This is the darkness I carried, but God is so, so good that He revealed His goodness and all these promises we have reviewed up until now. This is why I am passionate about the Word because He is faithful and true; the Word is something to stand on.

Back to this disappointment issue, which, may I remind you, is only a dark point of view. Because of the perspective from hell, I not only let many of my dreams die but some I killed very dramatically and buried them. God knew where they were. God sees everything, which means He saw me start killing myself as I suffocated these dreams. So when I came to these promises of life, I knew that I had to let some things die to receive the life Jesus had for me. I had to get rid of the lies I had partnered up with that gave the enemy the right to kill, steal, and destroy me.

Jesus has already walked this walk. God revealed that as I walk with Him, I surrender and give pain to Him; it is not for me to carry the burdens or the death any longer. He took it all on the cross, and He wants it once and for all. The pain we carry, we are to give to Him because He took it for us. By the way, this is also for you; as you walk with Him, you get to give Him your pain, your suffering, your worries, your death, everything.

I want to remind you that when Jesus went to the cross, we know He died. He died—His life gone. But on the third day, He ROSE AGAIN, and He came back in the resurrection power; HE came back to life with—and in—all the fullness of power and authority. With even more praise and excitement, I share what He shared with me—this is *exactly* what is happening in your life! You are coming back to life in the fullness of His power, His authority, His boldness, His Joy, His peace, His life—life to the fullest.

Look up what John 12:24 explains, and answer this: What does it mention has to happen to the grain of wheat? And why must that happen?

Here is Jesus speaking about the need for grain to die in order to produce a bigger crop. Jesus goes on to explain about needing to lose your life or hate your life in this world for you to gain eternal life. I want to explain this a bit. We, you and I, are required to give up our lives, to die to this world, and to let our own ambitions and our own desires die in order to be born into the life of Jesus, to live the life HE has divinely designed for us. He wants us to live out the dreams beyond our own imagination so we may produce a crop bigger than what our own strength can produce.

Look up Colossians 2:20 and write it in the space below:

What truth! If we truly have died to the things of this world, then why do we allow the troubles of this world to weigh us down? Shouldn't we be walking with life? With joy no matter what? Here is a reminder I would speak over myself: "His life, not mine; His will, not mine; His love, not mine; His desire, not mine. His." I had to start to remind myself what Jesus has done. Being in Him, I have indeed died to this world and have become a creation of His, a heavenly creature. I live like a citizen of heaven because Jesus said that He came to give us life in the fullness of Him.

The God of love has pulled me out of death and into life. He pulled me out of the grave, out of despair and sorrow, and has given me His life to live.

Key to life is death—death to self, death to self-ambitions, self-promotion, self-everything—and giving it all to the Lord.

SURRENDERING

So how exactly are we to die to self? I mention death to life, but how exactly is this done? Here is one secret that is not so secret: we must surrender to die. For the most part, this word is not one to get people excited. Quite honestly, because it has a sense of defeat, it can be an undesirable thing to do for many. To surrender to God is the factor that will lead us to die to self. It is a surrendering of our past, our failures, our dreams, desires, gifts, talents, and surrendering our life to Him. We literally are saying, "I can't do this on my own—help!" We are also saying, "I trust you know better than I do." Otherwise, if we hold on, the past will keep us from coming into the fullness of God.

Let me share a day in my life when God was ever speaking and, thankfully, I was paying attention. We will go back to November of 2022. I was in a small town in Kentucky, a place I never knew existed, hosted by a wonderful family that carries the presence of the Lord and lives on an anointed land. I woke up one morning, went into the kitchen, and stared at the two-foot-tall scales used as decor. On the right side of the scale were two keys and, on the left, a dead ladybug and dust. I proceeded to get a napkin to clean out the dead bug and toss it in the garbage. As I went back upstairs, I suddenly felt an urge to go into the barn to dance! "It's foolish; I have a ton to do," I chided. Nevertheless, I proceeded to get dressed, go back downstairs, and grab the set of keys that rested on the right side of the scales. I walked outside and continued to the barn. I inserted the key and unlocked the joy of dancing. After about half an hour of dancing for my King and worshiping Him, I found myself on the floor, sitting with my knees up, staring outside the big barn door, gazing at the peaceful scenery. Uncontrollable weeping followed as I fell back, lay down, and tarried in tears. The laboring pain, the hurt I carried far too long, was replaced with the joy of life. Life was birthed that day. The womb of my spirit carried it, and it was heavy. It was as if I carried it as long as elephants do. The gestation period of elephants is close to twenty-two months; that is almost two years! I only pray that the promise I birthed is as big as an elephant.

I share this moment for a few reasons. First and foremost, I will admit that I never saw myself being in Kentucky; it was never on my radar. Many times, God will use the unthinkable to bring you through into your breakthrough; He will use the least of these. I say the least of these because the place He chose in Kentucky is a small town called Eastview, Kentucky, with a population of fewer than 2,500 people. This is the place God chose to bring Maritza back to life. For a girl who has always lived in the city, with the hustle and bustle of everyday life, God chose a small town to breathe new life into me.

Please understand that I seriously would have never chosen that place; I had to truly surrender to God for the place to live; I had to surrender my opinions; I had to surrender where I thought I was supposed to be. I promise you that small town now has a place in my heart, but I would have never come to have a newness in my perspective and in my being if I had not surrendered my life to God. There was so much surrendering in that season. I had to surrender even my own expectations of what I thought my life should look like by now—the timing, the whos, the whats, and the wheres.

Here is another brief but oh-so-powerful moment that occurred months after the barn. I was in Nepal on a mission trip. As we were worshiping one day after dinner, a song titled "I Surrender" came on, and instantly, I fell to my knees and knew there was more to surrender. There was stubbornness in me that needed to leave; it was an ugly stubbornness of being upset that I had not yet received my desires. Here I was, serving the King, but I still had some anger to let go, the loneliness to let go, more discouragement and disappointment. He showed me that He wanted to replace my heart with His; He wanted to give me His life, His perspective, but only by surrendering it ALL could I even receive His heart full of life.

For God to birth new life in you, know this: There must be a surrendering of something that gives life a chance.

I wonder if, even now, God is calling you to a "small town Kentucky" in your life—to slow down, give up control, and let Him do what He needs to do. I suggest if you want life, ask the following to the Lord: "Is there anything else that I need to surrender?"

KEYS BELONGING TO YOU

Another revelation God shared with me that day in "small town" Kentucky involved the scales. Scales represent justice. When I look back at this moment, I recall that on one side of the scales was death. On the other, the keys that lead to life being birthed. Before I move forward to this revelation, I must share with you about the keys that God has already given you, keys that belong to us as children of God.

Read the following scriptures, and next to them, write what keys are discussed.

Matthew 16:19 ______________________________

Revelation 1:18 ______________________________

I can't emphasize enough about these keys. First of all, yes, keys to the kingdom of heaven. We have access to the kingdom of God in heavenly places. As for the keys explained in Revelation, these are the keys I want to take a moment to consider with you because of the magnitude of power they carry. In this place of Scripture, John is having an encounter with the resurrected Christ, the Son of Man dressed in a long robe with a gold sash wrapped around His chest, hair like wool, eyes like fiery flame, feet like fine bronze, and a voice like the sound of cascading waters as Jesus tells Him, "I am the First and the Last, and the Living One. I was dead, but look—I am alive forever and ever, and I hold the keys of death and Hades." I pray you get this. Here we have Jesus, who is in us, and we are in Him, and HE HOLDS the keys to death and Hades. As we have mentioned, He is the One who told us that everything that is His is also ours. Let me just print it out: We, as heirs, hold the keys to death and Hades when we *truly* walk in Him.

The authority we carry with these keys is beyond our own comprehension. I remember when I was working at the bank, I had access to areas that the public didn't. That is the kind of access you have with the keys Jesus gives. Just like Isaiah 22:22 declares, "I will place the key of the House of David on his shoulder; what he opens, no one can close; what he closes, no one can open." We are the ones who can open and close doors, and when we do, no one else can open or close them.

Back to the scales in Kentucky, which held death and keys to life. What the Lord told me that day after I had my encounter with Him was, "Maritza, the keys were available to you; only YOU had to physically grab them and then proceed to the door that the keys opened. THEN you still had to physically insert the key and unlock the door." As I listened, He further explained: "Just as I have given you the keys to the kingdom of heaven, and those of death and Hades, they are worthless if you don't take action and actually use them."

I am going to say this and move on. If you truly believe Jesus has given you the keys to the kingdom, and He is in you and you in Him, it is time for you to start using them. Start asking Him more questions about spiritual matters and how these keys work. Far too long has the church allowed death to strike and be beaten by it. It is time for us to take the authority Jesus gives us and start bringing life into this realm—not just life but *zoe* life, meaning life possessed by a divine being. "God raised Him up, ending the pains of death, because it was not possible for Him to be held by it" (Acts 2:24). Living in Him allows us to not be held down by death any longer. New life and new beginnings are at your disposal.

BREATH OF LIFE

Though I spoke about the keys the Lord has given us, I can feel many of you reading this have been or still are in a place where you have been suffocating, gasping for air to stay alive, maybe even thinking you don't have the strength to take another step. Possibly, it is apathy, the life stealer, that is slowly taking breath away from you.

Here is good news for you: "Then the Lord God formed the man out of the dust from the ground and breathed the breath of life into his nostrils, and the man became a living being." (Genesis 2:7). Though God has already breathed His breath of life into you, He is doing it again; He is breathing afresh into your lungs. It is the second wind that is coming over you, just as a runner gets a second wind in a long race. The breath of life is moving into your lungs at this very moment; all you need to do is breathe in deep.

Just think of how God is the One who gave you life. When He created Adam, God breathed THE BREATH OF LIFE into his nostrils. You have the very breath of God as a human being. Why would He let you suffocate now?

He is life, and He is for you. It is time that you rise up and fill your lungs with praise so you can take the keys He has given you and use them. He wants to give you His breath so you may be able to run your race full force, fully alive, with the full power and authority of life He has given you with the keys.

THE FULLNESS OF LIFE

> Made us alive with the Messiah even though we were dead in trespasses. You are saved by grace. —Ephesians 2:5

If only you knew what an honor it has been to walk with you throughout this journey, sharing what Jesus wants you to know. He has conquered death, and death cannot have you! Once again, Jesus in John 10:10 says that He came to give us life in its fullness. When we understand this promise of life, all other parts of the fullness we get by being in Him just fall into place; it is the one that overflows with all of the gifts we get and attributes of our Father.

Earlier in this section, I shared Revelation 1:18, where Jesus spoke, saying He is the "Living One." I want to cover more about this. The Lord Himself wants you and I to understand that we have His life in Him. To explain this, I want to cover the scriptures that precede Jesus speaking; I want to share the words that describe how John saw Jesus.

> And among the lamp stands was One like the Son of Man, dressed in a long robe and with a gold sash wrapped around His chest. His head and hair were white like wool—white as snow—and His eyes like a fiery flame. His feet were like fine bronze as it is fired in a furnace, and His voice like the sound of cascading waters. He had seven stars in His right hand; a sharp double-edged sword came from His mouth, and His face was shining like the sun at midday." —Revelation 1:13-16

I bring this up because something the Lord informed me while on the mission field in Nepal is that we are to have this same life of the resurrected Jesus—the same power. As we read that passage, we see the holiness over His head, the purity of His clothing, the eyes of fire, of fiery love for His people, the voice of healing and power, along with His face brilliantly shining. Can you remember the last time you saw your face in the mirror when it was full of joy radiating like the glory of the Lord? This is the kind of life we have access to, not just the human Jesus life, which absolutely is amazing, but we also have the life of the *resurrected Jesus.*

Find Colossians 1:19 and write it in the space below:

Life to the fullness is being filled with Him, in Him, by Him—living a life full of His everlasting life and all He has died to give you. As you yourself wrote that verse out, you can witness that it is God's pleasure to have filled Jesus with His fullness. And it was God who so loved you that He sent His one and only Son, and when you believe in Him, you receive everlasting life. When you walk in Him, the fullness of God is in you!

TIME TO EXPLODE

There is a bursting of new life! As I asked the Lord how He wanted to end this section, I kept hearing, "Remind them to enjoy life. The wild is to be released; Holy Spirit in you is wild and not to be limited. Adventure is in Him because the Holy Spirit is wild and untamed."

It is time to get excited for life, to dream again, and to be in expectation. There is dynamite in the Spirit, and it is about to explode with unshakable joy and life. You are wild and free—free to dance, free to sing, and free to be the person He created you to be. You are no longer bound by the chains of death but alive in Him. Look up the following promises and find the truth of life in them.

Colossians 3:3 ____

Prov 8:35 ____

If you are alive, breathing, and able to open your mouth, it is time to praise the Lord! Time to keep dancing and dreaming. This is how I envision what being alive and staying in the glory realm, in the spirit realm, and in the heavenly realm of Jesus is like. The last thing about this explosion of life I kept hearing in the Spirit is this: "Seek Holy Spirit! Seek Holy Spirit!"

Life, the fullness of life, is yours for the taking.

Join me and put on your dancing shoes, turn on the music, turn on the joy, and dance your heart out like no one is watching except for your King, the Living One. Here is a song you can dance to; it's called "RU Ready" by Godfrey Birtill. Are you ready?! Let's dance, for we are alive in Him!

> I have been crucified with Christ and I no longer live, but Christ lives in me. The life I now live in the body, I live by faith in the Son of God, who loved me and gave Himself for me. —Galatians 2:19-20

PRAYER

Jesus, thank you that you came to give me life, life in its fullness and life everlasting. Today, I ask that you reveal anything that I need to surrender to you that is keeping me from receiving the life you came to give me. Help me surrender completely to you. I choose life today, in Jesus' name. Amen.

CHAPTER 10

REMAIN IN HIM

Remain in Me, and I in you. Just as a branch is unable to produce fruit by itself unless it remains on the vine, so neither can you unless you remain in Me. —John 15:4

It is finished. So what exactly was finished again? We are at the end of this book, yet at times, the question rests. Though this was covered when we first started this book, here it is: The battle in your mind, the battle for your soul, the battle for your identity—it is finished. It is established in the heavens; you have been made new in Christ Jesus. With the same power that raised Him from the dead and seated Him in the heavens (Ephesians 1:20), you too, are able to walk in this as a citizen of heaven. "But our citizenship is in heaven, from which we also eagerly wait for a Savior, the Lord Jesus Christ" (Philippians 3:20). He has come, He is alive, and we are to bring heaven on earth. The only way to do so is by walking and living our lives as citizens of heaven.

Scripture tells us exactly how to remain; our job is to pay attention and be doers of the Word, not just listeners or readers. We are to be the living Word, just as Jesus is the living Word. Look at the scripture that blatantly tells us how we know we are in Him. This is also how we have come to this living life of being in Him. Read the following scriptures and write how they tell us we are to remain in Him.

1 John 2:5-6 ______________________________

1 John 4:13 ______________________________

Walk as He did.

WALK IN HIM

When it comes to walking, Scripture gives us many examples of what it means to walk in Christ. Here are some scriptures for you to look up; next to them, write what each verse tells us we must walk in. I will do the first one for all of us.

Ephesians 5:2 Walk in LOVE

Ephesians 5:8 ______

Ephesians 5:15 ______

1 John 1:7 ______

Galatians 5:16 ______

Colossians 1:10 ______

Take note of what we should be walking in, which these scriptures give us, for all of them are important! There is one in particular that has always grabbed my attention, and that is "walk in love." Here is another verse to solidify walking in love is remaining in Him: "And we have come to know and to believe the love that God has for us. God is love, and the one who remains in love remains in God, and God remains in Him" (1 John 4:16). I couldn't have said it better.

We want to walk in love because God is love, in Him! Read the following Bible sections: John 15:9-13, Ephesians 4:17-5:21, Romans 6:4.

What we just read in John is so powerful because it establishes love—love that Jesus has for you and what it looks like to love God and others! To love Jesus is to follow His commands, to be doers of His Word. To love others means to lay down your own life for your friends. I'll be honest: I haven't had many people lay down their lives for me. We live in a world so full of selfishness that many don't have the capacity to think outside of themselves. But you do now! Let me tell you, I promise you, I am not a fan of writing; it takes time. But I love you so much I want to see you step into your destiny. I laid down my life to be sitting and typing away. It is because He first loved me—and I want you to come to know His love.

As for the excerpt in Ephesians, I can't even begin—the Word is enough. This section is so rich! It's like chocolate and wine together, speaking about how we are to think differently, act differently, talk differently, and be kind and compassionate, forgiving others. It teaches us how we must be alert and awake, staying in the light, not getting drunk but instead being filled continually by the Spirit, speaking in psalms, hymns, and spiritual songs! This reminds me of releasing our sound, the sound of joy, yet also still submitting to one another in the fear of Christ. Again, we are to sound like Him, walk like Him, talk like Him. We are heirs of the throne, letting go of all this world because if we are still in the world (walking like them, talking like them), then we can't inherit the kingdom. But we are to walk in love; it is our new normal. We can walk in the power of God and the fullness of what He has for us.

> Therefore, as you have received Christ Jesus the Lord, walk in Him, rooted and built up in Him and established in the faith, just as you were taught, overflowing with gratitude. —Colossians 2:6–7

It is in walking with Jesus, in His fellowship, in the relationship with Him, that we grow into allowing our hearts to be taken captive by Him, and we learn to walk completely in Him. In the walking, we are established in the faith; in the walking, we overflow with gratitude because of His love for us. In the walking, we gain trust and become rooted in His love. This is when we allow Him to love us, and we are captivated by Him, and, in return, we love on Him. This is the only way we will be able to be doers of His Word and not just make reading the Word something to check off a list. Along with this, I want to share a few more ways that will help us remain in Him.

Look up the following scriptures and write what they tell us to do:

Psalm 119:11 ______________________________

Proverbs 7:2-3 ______________________________

Proverbs 3:1–2 ______________________________

Deuteronomy 11:18 ______________________________

2 Corinthians 3:3 ______________________________

It is by staying close to Him and being in the Word that we may be doers of the Word. These scriptures are so beautiful to me—so beautiful, yet so important. It is important that we let Him write His commands, His Word, in our hearts. It is all about the position of our hearts when it comes to abiding in Him. Matthew 6:21 says, "Where your treasure is, there your heart will be also."

God has always been after our hearts. We must allow Him to write not only His commands on our hearts but also His words of eternity.

THE FULLNESS GIVEN

The shift that will take us back to the Garden, back to the beginning where nothing else matters but Him, is making Him our one and utmost desire. This means seeking Him always in everything and making our act of faith be to seek Him, seek His face, seek Holy Spirit, where our eyes are locked on His because, as we have walked with Him, we have become enamored. We have come to know Him and His true colors, faithful and true. It is here we begin to receive the fullness of Him, our inheritance. Himself in us and us in Him, carrying His character, His fruit, His desires.

Jesus came not just to die and give us salvation, but He came to give Himself to His bride, to His people, to you and me. When we remain, the reward is the fullness of God. Find the following scriptures and notice the loaded promise they give.

Colossians 2:9-10 ______________________________

Ephesians 3:19 ______________________________

Scripture, the Holy Bible itself—Jesus Himself since He is the Word—says that He wants to fill us with all HIS fullness; in fact, per the verse in Colossians we just read, He already has filled us! The fullness of God is for us. It is available for us if we believe!

"Now without faith it is impossible to please God, for the one who draws near to Him must believe that He exists and rewards those who seek Him [diligently]" (Hebrews 11:6, parenthetical mine). This is our reward.

One thing for sure I say to you: I believe this and receive it; I believe He wants to give me the fullness of Him. If you are still reading these pages, I assume you are hungry for that, too, for the fullness. Keep pressing in, and don't stop. Don't ever stop. His Word is a promise, and you can take those promises to the bank of heaven. Take them as you remain and keep growing in Him.

The only way we will come to this is if we never quit, if we stay the course, and if we keep seeking His face. We want to be the ready virgins, ready and full of the oil—those who did not have to leave the premises to go looking for what was already in us. We must remain.

ABIDE

To remain is to abide; to abide is to remain. What does this really mean? What does it look like? How can we really remain? This word is so weighty. It makes me smile because that is what it is to stay in the glorious, weighty presence of God. When I first came to the Lord, there was a pastor in Texas who I was led to learn from. He read out of the King James Version Bible, and to this day, I can hear his voice reading and preaching on John 15:7: "If ye abide in me, and my words abide in you, ye shall ask what ye will, and it shall be done unto you." My personal Bible uses the word "remain" instead of "abide." But since I hear the voice of Papa T in my mind, when I think of Him in us, His Word in us, Jesus in us, I decided to understand the word "abide."

When looking into the usage of John 15:4 and 15:7, the root word comes from the Greek word *meno*, which primarily means "to stay in a given place, state relation or expectancy." It goes on to explain it further as "to continue, dwell, endure, be present, remain, stand, tarry." Looking at the definitions of this Greek word, there were a few that stood out, and one, of course, is the word *remain*, which led me to the same root word of meno. With that, I want to emphasize how it mentions it primarily means "to stay in a given place." When I hear this, I hear "to stay in the Word," but I also hear "to stay in the presence of God."

This leads to the other word that captured my attention: dwell. When I hear this word, I think of two verses:

> The one who lives under the protection of the Most High dwells in the shadow of the Almighty. —Psalm 91:1

> I have asked one thing from the Lord; it is what I desire: to dwell in the house of the Lord all the days of my life, gazing on the beauty of the Lord and seeking Him in His temple. —Psalm 27:4

Honestly, I feel these two verses really do the job of showing what the word dwell really represents. Nevertheless, I will expand. A dwelling place is a home. My *Vine's Concise Dictionary* states that one of the definitions for the word abide is abode. Look, I mentioned in a previous section that we are citizens of heaven, which means that our *abode*, our dwelling place, our home, is in heaven—in Christ Jesus, in Him.

I am not done with the word dwell, so bear with me because the rest of this is beyond wonderful. I want to take you deep into His truth so you may rise up in the Spirit and dwell in these heavenly places. As I kept on digging for the meaning of the word dwell, I found a golden nugget: the word "to marry." Yes, you saw that right; it comes from the Hebrew word *yashab*, which means "to sit down." This word was used in the Old Testament to describe one who is to sit down and assume the throne! Did you catch that? To assume the throne. In essence, this word also means "to begin to reign." Okay, I want to tie this together for you because this is really what Jesus wants us to grasp, which is our true position and identity. This word to *dwell* or *abide* is to marry and take a seat. You see, we are His bride, and we are to take our rightful seat with the King on the throne! This question remains: Have you said yes to His proposal?

It is in abiding and in dwelling in Him that we are captivated by Him and fall in love with Him. When we finally say yes to His proposal to be His bride, we can sit confidently at His right hand—in Him. We can assume our throne and begin to reign. When we say yes to His love, yes from the bride to the bridegroom, we come to the chambers of the throne; we become one and sit and reign together. I briefly mentioned in the section on peace how being at peace comes from a Greek word that means "to join" and "to set at one again." To abide and to be at peace go hand in hand. When we abide, we are at peace; we are joined to the bridegroom, our King, and taken back to our original position before the foundations of the world. Just as a husband and wife become one, we become one with Him. We are joined to Him sitting on the throne. This is what dwelling means. To dwell in the house of the Lord all the days of our lives!

TAKE YOUR SEAT

In case you are still pondering, "So how do we remain in Him?" read the following verse:

> He raised us up with Christ the exalted One, and we ascended with him into the glorious perfection and authority of the heavenly realm, for we are now co-seated as one with Christ! —Ephesians 2:6 TPT

This is how we remain in Him. WE TAKE OUR SEATS!

In this journey, we walk as He did, just as we covered in this section already. BUT there comes a time as we mature when we must really believe we are seated with Him in the heavenly places, and we must take our seat. This is where we reign, being one with Him.

I'm going to share a moment: I was praying outdoors, staring at a bonfire created for us to stay warm. As I prayed, I stared. As I stared, I couldn't help but be mesmerized by the fire. Then I started to gaze at the very center of the fire—the part where I could see blue, turquoise, and purple flames. I loved watching this fire dance and, even more so, watching the colors and the wood at the core glowing like gold. As I contemplated, the Lord started to speak to me. Now, I knew that what I was staring at was the hottest part of the fire; the hottest part is not the orange flames, in case you didn't know. The Lord started to mention how that part of the fire is who I am—the hottest, the part closest to the source, the one that creates the flames. I was in awe of this. Then, a few days after this happened, I described this encounter with a friend who happens to be a firefighter. You know what he said? He shared with me the part of the fire I was describing is called the "seat" of the fire. As soon as I heard that, I heard God say, "It is time to take your seat!"

I don't want to take too much time with this, but I do feel it is essential. There is so much about fire. First, fire purifies; in certain areas of the world, it is used to burn garbage; sometimes, it forges diamonds; it purifies. There are two kinds of fire we are dealing with here. One is the fire that the devil throws at us to make us withdraw from our calling. We can read about this in the book of Daniel and the furnace, where we read that the "enemy" even called out for the heat to be turned up seven times the normal.

The other kind of fire? Go to the following scriptures and write down what fire is described.

1 Kings 18:38 ______________________________

Hebrews 12:29 ______________________________

There is a fire from heaven, a fire that is sent from God meant to purify you and not take you out. This fire is meant to consume you, to make you burn with life and passion. Interestingly, fire requires a source of energy, just like us, in order to stay alive. God is the source of energy to us, the oxygen, and the breath of life.

"He raised us with him, and we are sitting with him in heaven in Jesus the Messiah." (Ephesians 2:6 ARTB). As you allow that fire to consume you, you become that burning fire in heavenly places; your essence becomes His essence. The hottest part of the fire is where we become one with Him, and we learn to take our seat.

I want to share a portion of my dream about this. In a dream, I was getting food with a friend, and as we were ready to sit to eat, all of a sudden, in my dream, I was in a vehicle driving. More happened in the dream, but I want to highlight the way this dream ended. I was angry and threw everything in my hand on the floor in a temper tantrum, including my Bible, and said to my friend, "I am not eating." After I paused and looked at my possessions on the floor, I apologized to my friend, saying, "I am sorry," and I proceeded to pick up my Bible and express, "I am still not eating."

As this dream was interpreted to me, I was shown I never sat down. I went straight into a vehicle. This dream ended with me being upset, saying I was not eating, revealed I didn't proceed to sit at the table. When I had this dream, I was in a season of much frustration, feeling so lost, and honestly feeling I didn't belong anywhere. I kept running away from those who loved me because I feared they didn't want me, I feared I was a burden, and I feared I was unwanted and had no place. I was unable to rest, unable to sit.

I will pose a question: Is this you? Are you in a place where you keep running from place to place, trying to find where you belong? Are you not sitting and taking your place? I am telling you now that God is saying, "Take your seat!" Take your seat not just at the table but on your throne. Jesus gave you that seat at the cross, in the heavenlies. If you abide in Him and He in you, then you are surely on that throne—IF you take your seat!

Well, Maritza, what do you mean take the throne? You were just talking about fire. Indeed, I was—the seat of the fire.

Look up Daniel 7:9 and write it below:

Now find Ezekiel 1:4 and 1:25-27 and describe the throne in your own words.

You see, the throne we sit on is a throne of fire. Brother, sister, when you feel the battle is heating up, that the fire of the enemy has been increased, remember that we have the hottest seat in the house!

TIME TO RULE AND REIGN

It is time for the sons and daughters to take their seats, to rule and reign—to take dominion of the earth, to take territory and stop allowing the devil to terrorize and continue to blaspheme the house of the Lord.

"You must go from sword to scepter." This truth impacted me so much, and it helped me realize the importance of taking our seat. At the moment, I honestly cannot remember who said this; I wish I did so I could give credit where credit is due. There is such power on the seat; after I heard this, I had to look into what makes a scepter so powerful over a sword. This was very important for me to know because I am all about the slaying of giants. As a matter of fact, I am reading a book called *How to Field Dress a Giant* while I am in the process of writing this book. That book talks about David, who was a true warrior, yet he was also a king! So what is it about a scepter that holds more power than a sword?

There are some quite amazing findings about this scepter. Here are a few. The scepter has been described as a stick for punishing, writing, fighting, ruling, and walking (this would be a staff). It is a baton of ROYALTY—a scepter is held by one in royalty. The scepter itself is a weapon; a word I came across is *a cudgel*—that is, a stick used as a weapon. It is also a verb, which means "to beat." A scepter can, indeed, be used to beat the opponent. So rest assured that when you hold a scepter, you still have a weapon.

I won't stop there because the rest is amazing on the deeper meaning of the scepter! Let's read the following scriptures: "Your throne, God, is forever and ever; the scepter of Your kingdom is a scepter of justice" (Psalm 45:6) and "Your throne, God, is forever and ever, and the scepter of Your kingdom is a scepter of justice" (Hebrews 1:8).

What is the one word that is used in both these scriptures telling us what this scepter is?

Notice in these verses it mentions this is the Lord's scepter! So when we talk about this scepter, it is not any normal earthly scepter; it is one that holds a power that is greater than any on this earth. That scepter is the scepter of justice, which God gives to those who are obedient. When we hold the scepter, we hold justice! The Lord calls out the truth and roars the thunders of justice from His throne, with us being one with Him. He calls us to voice justice on earth as we are sitting on that throne holding our scepters.

If that isn't enough, because it isn't, let's cover the next reason a scepter is powerful. To understand, look up and read Esther 4:11 and 5:1-2. After reading Esther, in your own words, write how you would describe the meaning of the scepter.

In awe, after I read these scriptures during my study on a scepter, I acknowledged how powerful the scepter is. Here, in these verses of the living Word, we see a scepter holds life and death. Raising the scepter gives life to the person before it; otherwise, if that scepter remains low—whether on the lap or the side of the throne, wherever it was kept—it means death. Brother, sister, when you hold the scepter, for those warriors out there, just like a sword, you carry life and death in your hands.

Wow, if you are not amazed, I don't know what to say. The kind of power Jesus gives us, where He gave us HIS everything, words escape me on how magnificent our God is! I am going to cover one last thing as we end this journey on these pages. The journey never ends, and I really believe God will continue to show you more as you abide in Him.

Something I love about the Word of God—besides the fact of it being the living Word of Jesus Himself—is, yes, it is a book to teach us so we may learn from those people in the Bible. I want to briefly share how God was speaking clearly about learning from Moses. In the journey out of Egypt, there were two instances where the community was with no water. The Israelites began to grumble and complain. In Exodus 17:5-7, God told Moses to strike the rock, and water would come out. The next time this happened, God told him to speak to the rock. Go and read the story for yourself in Numbers 20:1-12, paying extra attention to verses 6 through 12, then write out verse 12 below.

I'll be honest: My heart sank when I read verse 12. It was my heart crying that I may not fall into the same place as Moses. I want to trust the Lord with ALL my heart. As I read this story with fresh eyes, and why I am sharing this now, my prayer for you is that you may come to the place of trusting God in such a way that if He says speak, you speak with the full authority He has given you. The authority a king possesses by sitting on the throne is that you may just speak and not have to strike. The first time God told Moses to strike the rock was when they were walking together, and that is where Moses' faith was. The second time around, God TRUSTED Moses to be able to SPEAK instead of striking the rock; this was a new level of faith.

The power that was given to him is the same power in Jesus. This is where God wants us to be—to speak and not have to strike anymore, the same power that raised Jesus from the grave, the same power from Genesis 1 where God spoke and creation manifested! He spoke. Just one word can change the trajectory of this life on earth. We are sitting on the throne with Him, and He wants us to TRUST Him so much that we follow His direction and can just speak, and when we do so, we can manifest just as He did.

Look, when we abide, when we dwell and sit on the throne of heaven with Jesus, IN HIM—that same Creator of heaven and earth is in us who is ruling and reigning. We can raise a scepter and speak with authority, and when the sound is released from our mouths, it moves mountains.

Can you trust Him now? Will you trust Him? When nothing makes sense, will you trust Him? Will you shake the darkness to bring light onto the earth? Will you bring heaven on earth now? Will you believe and speak? Will you believe now that you are seated? Will you take that seat on the throne now? Will you rule and reign with the Creator of heaven and earth? Are you ready to start living the life you were originally created to live in the Garden, in the throne room, in the heavenly realm with the fullness of God?

> I no longer live, but Christ lives in me. The life I now live in the body, I live by faith IN THE SON OF GOD, who loved me and gave Himself for me. — Galatians 2:20 (emphasis mine)

PRAYER

Jesus. I thank you that you gave yourself for me so that I may live the life you created me to live. I want to dwell in you all the days of my life. I choose to believe that you have given me all power, authority, and dominion to live the life of ruling and reigning. I choose to take the seat that you gave me, Jesus, the hottest seat in the house, which is your throne, to sit with you in heaven as you mention in Ephesians. That same power that resurrected you has given me the life to sit with you and rule and reign, now on earth as it is in heaven. Thank you, Jesus, for your life that I now live by faith in you. Amen.

MEET THE AUTHOR

Maritza Barron is a woman who has decided to live a surrendered life to God in all areas. Rooted in Christ, her mission is to share the unfailing love of Jesus. She is called to bring freedom in Christ to the nations, to share the gospel, and to bring change to the world through the power of the Holy Spirit and the faithful love of God. Maritza's passion is to see people's lives transformed through the Word and for them to encounter the love of the living God.

ALSO BY MARITZA BARRON

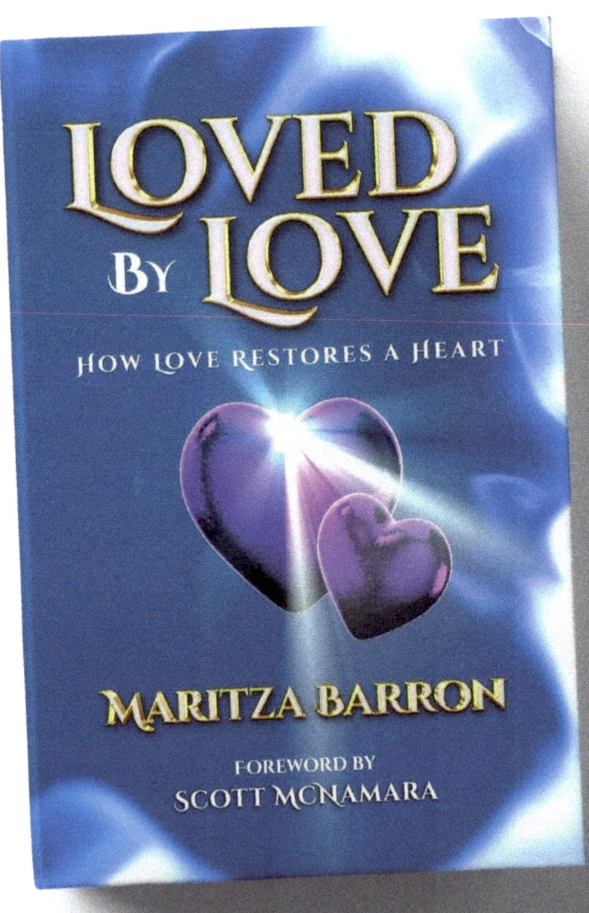

AVAILABLE ON AMAZON

LEADER GUIDE

I want to let you know I am so proud of you for stepping into your call to lead a group. May you be blessed and emboldened in this time. May grace and wisdom come over you as you help others grow in Him.

These are suggestions for each time you meet. You will see the suggested questions for the session you are on. As you go through the questions and time sharing, I highly recommend you use this time to minister to the people if they expose struggles and pray for them. Remember, always make room for the Holy Spirit AND have fun!!

WHEN YOU MEET:

1. Give time to greet each other.

2. Open with prayer. Inviting the Holy Spirit to the gathering. Asking Him for revelation.

3. Pick questions to ask, or go through all of them, if time allows, for the session you are on.

FAITH

1. When it comes to the word "wait" from the different translations of scripture, which word struck you most and why?

2. What promises are you carrying?

3. What seed has been planted in you that God is asking you to grow?

4. What is God asking you to do by faith?

PEACE

1. Have you been speaking words that have been bringing death to your life?

2. After looking at the definitions of peace, how would you now describe peace? What is that peace that Jesus came to give us?

3. Which of the definitions of peace struck your heart most and why?

4. Is there anything you need or any place you have felt unsettled that you would be willing to share and give to Jesus?

LEADER GUIDE

JOY

1. Have you been overlooking the joy in the journey? Have you been walking from point A to point B missing out on the flowers?

2. What are some of the blessings and the fruit around you that you can be thankful for?

3. Have you been in the midst of sorrow and tears? What place of sorrow are you needing Him to come in and hear the words "Why are you crying," followed by joy?

4. There is value inside of you, you are needed, and your sound is needed. What area in your life is God asking you to see the value you carry?

RIGHTEOUS

1. Was there anything in 1 Corinthians that you felt convicted with? If so, are you willing to repent and take the time to confess? (If you do so with others, firstly, know I am proud of you, secondly know your healing is available.)

2. Did you accept the invitation given in Isaiah 1:18? If so, what did the Lord share with you?

3. You learn you have been given access to the throne room through the blood, do you run to the Father with confidence or are you still feeling you cannot come before Him? If you feel you are unable to go to the throne room, why?

4. You have been declared righteous, blessed, holy, and blameless. Are you able to thank Him for this and walk in it?

INHERITANCE

1. What does your mind think about most?

2. Have you been partnering with poverty and fear of not having enough?

3. Did you take your seat at the banquet table and what are you reaching for on this table- what are you going to eat to be satisfied?

4. God wants to give you your inheritance through obedience. Is there an area you have been asked to be obedient?

5. Do you know who God is for you? And do you know who you are in Him?

WISDOM

1. Do you relate to the logic being a hindrance to trusting God?

2. What is your favorite part of Revelation Ch 4?

3. Psalm 37 starts with instructing us to not envy. Do you struggle with envy/ jealousy? If so, did you ask the Father why and where this is coming from?

4. If you are asking for wisdom, do you feel there is any double mindedness? Is there anywhere you can worship God more?

LEADER GUIDE

CONFIDENCE

1. What part of the covenant readings grabbed your attention, or was highlighted to you in which the Lord wants you to grasp?

2. What are some good things you remember that God has done for you?

3. Name some characteristics of the Lord that you can stand on, and why?

4. Do you still feel like there are times you walk in the orphan mindset? If so, why?

LIFE

1. Has disappointment been a blinder in your life? If so, what is that disappointment and what promise does God have for you?

2. What are you needing to surrender to God so that you may step into the fullness of His life for you?

3. You have been given keys by the King; have you been walking around not using them? If so, how is God asking you to use them?

4. Can you remember the last time you saw your face in the mirror where it was full of joy radiating like the glory of the Lord?

REMAIN

1. Of the scriptures provided which tell us how to walk, which one do you feel you need to grow in? (Ephesians 5:2 - Walk in love; Ephesians 5:8 - Like children of light; Ephesians 5:15 - As wise; 1 John 1:7 - Walk in the light; Galatians 5:16 - By the Spirit; Colossians 1:10 - Worthy of the Lord.)

2. It is in the walking we overflow with gratitude and gain trust. Are these two areas that you feel you need to grow in, gratitude and trust? If so, what is one thing you are grateful for? What area do you feel you are unable to trust?

3. Have you said yes to His proposal? If not, what is keeping you from saying yes?

4. Are you in a place where you keep running from place to place trying to find where you belong? Are you not sitting and taking your place?

5. Are you ready to start living the life you were originally created to live, in the garden, in the throne room, in the heavenly realm with the fullness of God?

www.ingramcontent.com/pod-product-compliance
Ingram Content Group UK Ltd.
Pitfield, Milton Keynes, MK11 3LW, UK
UKHW062313290726
14090UKWH00018B/1044

9 798986 306223